DAVID & MEREDITH LIB

KNOW BETTER, DO BETTER

COMPREHENSION

Fueling the Reading Brain With Knowledge, Vocabulary, and Rich Language

SCHOLASTIC

To all the teachers who, in the hardest of times,
continue to give so much so generously

Senior Vice President and Publisher: Tara Welty
Editorial Director: Sarah Longhi
Development Editor: Raymond Coutu
Production Editor: Danny Miller
Assistant Editor: Samantha Unger
Creative Director: Tannaz Fassihi
Interior Designer: Maria Lilja

Scholastic is not responsible for the content of third-party websites and does not endorse any site or imply that the information on the site is error-free, correct, accurate, or reliable.

Photos ©: Cover: Shutterstock.com; 10: Jim Craigmyle/Getty Images; 13: FatCamera/Getty Images; 17: sanjeri/Getty Images; 23: SolStock/Getty Images; 32: Maskot/Getty Images; 56: FatCamera/Getty Images; 65: PixelCatchers/Getty Images; 69, 72, 73, 81: iStock/Getty Images; 70: Hill Street Studios/Getty Images; 74: Tim Platt/Getty Images; 86: fstop123/Getty Images; 88: Andersen Ross Photography Inc./Getty Images; 100: sanjeri/Getty Images; 116: Maskot/Getty Images; 130: LWA/Dann Tardif/Getty Images. Classroom photos provided by StandardsWork, Inc. and the Knowledge Matters Campaign. All remaining photos © Shutterstock.com and Scholastic Inc.

Excerpts from: "Jabberwocky" from *Through the Looking-Glass* by Lewis Carroll, 1871; "Author Profile: Rick Riordan" © Scholastic Inc.; *Missing May* © 1992 by Cynthia Rylant. Used by permission of Scholastic Inc.; "The Fisherman and His Wife" by the Brothers Grimm, 1812; *The Great Fire* © 1995 by Jim Murphy. Used by permission of Scholastic Inc.; *Esperanza Rising* © 2000 by Pam Muñoz Ryan. Used by permission of Scholastic Inc.; *Owen and Mzee* © 2006 by Turtle Pond Publications LLC and Lafarge Eco Systems Ltd. Used by permission of Scholastic Inc.; "The Spirit of Liberty" speech by Judge Learned Hand, 1944; *Lety Out Loud* © 2019 by Angela Cervantes. Used by permission of Scholastic Inc.; "Sentence Expansion" from *The Writing Revolution* by Judith C. Hochman and Natalie Wexler © 2017 by The Writing Revolution. Used by permission of John Wiley & Sons, Inc. All rights reserved.

2 3 4 5 6 7 8 9 10 11   40   33 32 31 30 29 28 27 26 25 24

Scholastic Inc., 557 Broadway, New York, NY 10012

CONTENTS

Acknowledgments 5

Foreword by Margaret G. McKeown 6

Introduction 8

PART I: WHAT KIDS NEED TO KNOW TO COMPREHEND TEXTS

CHAPTER 1: The Role of Knowledge 18

CHAPTER 2: Vocabulary: Meaningful Words 38

CHAPTER 3: Morphology and Etymology:
            The Structure and Origin of Words 55

PART II: WHAT YOU NEED TO KNOW TO FUEL THE READING BRAIN

CHAPTER 4: Comprehension: An Overview 66

CHAPTER 5: Comprehension: A Deep Dive 71

PART III: WHAT YOU CAN DO TO FUEL THE READING BRAIN

CHAPTER 6: The Power of Questions and Centering the Text 92

CHAPTER 7: The Power of Close Reading 111

CHAPTER 8: Writing to Learn, Writing to Comprehend 131

Conclusion 144

Resources 151

References 154

Index 158

"Reading comprehension is not an observable skill. It's not even a cluster of observable skills.... Cognitive scientists refer to comprehension as 'representation,' meaning it is represented in our minds as a set of understandings."

ACKNOWLEDGMENTS

We've learned *so* much from so many.

Foremost, the great Walter Kintsch. His patience with all our "what-if" and "what-about" questions knew no bounds. He died before this book came out; we hope he'd approve.

"Reading has a lot to do with words!" We're indebted to Chuck Perfetti for our deep understanding of that observation. His work with us in establishing the ladder of text complexity created the opening that helped move us away from the tyranny of leveled reading.

Chuck reintroduced us to Moddy McKeown, our keenest-eyed reader. We'll forever be grateful to Moddy for seeing what we were trying to do and claiming we accomplished it in her beautiful foreword. We were already big fans of her and Isabel Beck's sweeping body of work. Thank you.

We're grateful to Keith Stanovich who, with Anne Cunningham, penned the best title ever for a piece of reading research: "What Reading Does for the Mind." They established the importance of a volume of reading and how much it benefits even weak readers.

To E. D. Hirsch, first in the literacy world to insist on the key role knowledge has in literacy. He trod a rocky road and smoothed it for the rest of us.

Thanks to Sean Morrisey, who generously shared passion and ideas with us.

Hugs to our fellow Vermonters, Joey Hawkins and Diana Leddy, who have collaborated with us on some of the best work we've gotten to do. Chapter 8 exists because of Joey's feedback ("I know it's a reading book, but..."). They remind us writing and reading are forever intertwined.

Gratitude to Judith Hochman, first for Windward and helping us do better for our students and child. Then to Natalie Wexler and you for sharing those practices with the world.

To Lily Wong Fillmore for insisting English language learners have as much curiosity and language aptitude as anybody. Thank you for juicy sentences and so much more.

Eternal thanks to Sue Pimentel. Your dedication to equitable literacy and your friendship mean the world.

Hugs to our patient editor, Ray Coutu, who managed to deliver sharp feedback with a velvet touch.

To the talented educators who read early drafts closely: Julie Brown, Tori Filler, Callie Lowenstein, Jodi Rabat, Julie Robinson, and the oh-so-sharp crew at Imagine, Carey Swanson and April Thorburn. We appreciate you.

FOREWORD
by Margaret G. McKeown

I n this book, David and Meredith Liben gather the full force of their experience and knowledge to tackle the complex topic of reading comprehension. And they do it with aplomb, bringing wisdom and clarity to explanations of the reading brain's workings and recommendations for instruction.

David and Meredith are amazing educational professionals, not only because they have years of deep experience in teaching, school administration, and curriculum development, but also because they stay close to the research. They have investigative minds, realizing that knowing and understanding are ongoing processes. That spirit of investigation—that openness to *not* knowing, but working to find out—runs through what they have done in classrooms and what they recommend for teachers, including the approaches in this book.

A strong motivation for writing this book came from the Libens' deep concern that conversations about the science of reading (SOR) are dominated by foundational skills, and broader processes are being neglected. This book aims to change that by showing what else is crucial to reading success. Using clear, accessible language, the authors explain how processes work in the brain during reading, and how to use that understanding to create optimal instruction.

In the Introduction, they share an anecdote that illustrates how language comprehension processes are a natural part of how we make sense of the world. They make the point that reading instruction needs to be grounded in how comprehension actually occurs, rather than in isolated routines to apply to texts.

In Part I, the Libens lay the groundwork for comprehension with a discussion of the essential roles of knowledge and vocabulary. One notable knowledge-building recommendation is having all students at every reading level engage together in learning about the world. The authors explain how to build text sets that capture a range of complexities and allow even struggling readers to have access to the same core text as everyone else.

In their discussion of vocabulary, the authors explain why building depth, not just breadth, is essential and how both operate to ensure comprehension. A compelling aspect of their approach is placing awareness, investigation, and discovery at the heart of teaching vocabulary. They illustrate, through classroom anecdotes, how the best approach to promoting depth is devoting attention to, and use of, words throughout the school day.

In fact, throughout the book, the Libens offer wonderful peeks into classrooms. The vocabulary chapter opens with a lovely portrait of a word-focused community, along with an example of a word-focused read-aloud that makes me want to race out and discuss a good book with kids!

Part II focuses on the main attraction: comprehension. The foundation—for the Libens and for the field at large—is the Kintsch model of comprehension. That model is explored deeply and clearly here, taking the reader through concepts such as local and global cohesion, textbase, situation models, and standard of coherence, and showing how they matter to comprehension and instruction. They show how the processes that frame Kintsch's model can and should also frame instructional decisions related to comprehension.

At the heart of Part III is the Libens' version of close reading—a discussion-based, interactive approach, with artful questioning at its core, that aligns with the research on how reading processes work. *Artful* may sound daunting, but it means a simple pattern of following the ideas, information, and connections across a text.

The authors acknowledge a small role for standards and strategies, but explain that relying on them pulls attention away from the text and places it on the standard or strategy. The book's focus remains on how aspects of the comprehension process operate under real conditions, and they provide powerful examples of encounters with text—examples that are clearly grounded in the authors' experiences.

Know Better, Do Better: Comprehension offers a perfect balance of research findings, instructional recommendations, and suggestions for resources to build and enhance classroom reading experiences.

What makes the book refreshing to read, and valuable to classroom practice, is that the authors never lose sight of the goal of reading for understanding, and supporting students in doing that. And they emphasize the importance of undergirding that support with a sense of wonder and curiosity about the world, language, and what can be learned from reading.

—Margaret G. McKeown
Clinical Professor Emerita of Education, University of Pittsburgh
Member of the Reading Hall of Fame

Introduction

In the decade David was principal of the Family Academy, the public elementary school that we established in New York, he often took the M10 bus at 113th Street and 8th Avenue down to the district office. Meetings were always scheduled right after the school day started and during rush hour, which promised lots of interesting people and things to observe on the way.

One morning, David noticed a mother and daughter sitting near him. The little girl looked about age four, dressed for school as her mother was for work. At one point, the girl looked around, pointed to the sign over the windshield, and asked her mother, "What's that word after 'NO'?"

"Spitting," her mother responded.

"EWWWWW!" the girl said. After a minute of studying the sign and mouthing "no spitting," she went on, "You mean some people need to be TOLD that?", looking at her mother in disbelief. Clearly, this little girl came from a household where nobody had to be reminded that buses were not places to spit.

Her mother replied, "Yes. Some people haven't been taught not to spit in public."

A moment of silence passed while the girl absorbed that fact. Then she asked, "Who put that sign on the bus?"

The mother explained it probably wasn't the bus driver, but people who make the rules for the city, including the buses.

The girl, New York City kid that she was, announced, "I don't think a sign will stop people like that from spitting. Some kind of officer on the bus might, but not a sign!"

As they departed at the next stop, they left David thinking about their lively exchange.

Why are we telling you this story?

Fueled by her curiosity and the inquisitiveness nurtured by her mother, this preschooler had just engaged in many of the same activities that we use with students to achieve reading comprehension.

Let's take a look at what she did to comprehend the text over the windshield.

- First, she "read closely to determine what the text says." Sound familiar? That's because it appears in many standards documents and, more importantly, it is what proficient readers do to understand a text's message: read closely.
- Then she asked a clarifying question: "What's that word after 'NO'?" After being told the word in question was "spitting," she scowled and said "EWWWWW!" It's safe to say she was visualizing, another process that readers naturally do (and that we spend inordinate time trying to teach).
- Next, she asked, "You mean some people need to be TOLD that?" Here she was, once again, asking a question, and making a "text to knowledge" connection (e.g., no one in her world would do that).

- She then inferred there must be people in the world who weren't like her or people she knew—people who need to be told not to spit on the bus.
- Again, she asked another question: "Who put that sign on the bus?"
- Making yet another inference: If there are people who would spit on the floor of a city bus, a sign wouldn't stop them.
- This preschooler had synthesized so much information: If there's a "No Spitting" sign, some people must be spitting on a bus. But a sign won't work for those types of people, and a different solution to the problem is needed.

In a few short moments, she made a number of inferences, questioned the text and its premises, evaluated it critically, synthesized it, and came to a conclusion. She fully comprehended "no spitting," in other words. She didn't need strategy instruction, which has dominated comprehension instruction for nearly half a century. From working with and observing hundreds of children, we know they think strategically about a wide variety of things, all the time. So why do we still teach them, painstakingly, how to do that? This question will be explored more later.

Children are inferring all the time.

Why We Wrote This Book

In *Know Better, Do Better: Comprehension*, we show you how processes work in children's minds when they are reading. And we show you how to use that understanding to create conditions for every one of your students to experience seamless interactions with texts—texts far more complex and rich than "no spitting." We want your instruction to grow out of the research on how comprehension actually happens, which is not by having students learn and apply a bunch of isolated strategies.

"Reading comprehension" is a term we all use all the time in school. But what is it, really? And how do we ensure that all students achieve it? We wrote this book to answer those questions.

> We want your instruction to grow out of the research on how comprehension actually happens, which is not by having students learn and apply a bunch of isolated strategies.

How This Book Is Organized

Our discussion is structured this way:

- Part I focuses on the role of knowledge, vocabulary, morphology, and syntax, which, in essence, is an investigation of what lies underneath successful reading comprehension. We examine the importance of those ingredients and how to make sure you're teaching them in vibrant ways.

- Part II opens with a brief road map of the nature of reading comprehension, along with, in Chapter 4, a glossary of essential terms. In Chapter 5, we present the dominant research-based model of comprehension and what happens in the mind as we read. It's the essential information you need to become an informed and effective teacher of reading comprehension. It also sets you up to make the best use of the practical applications we recommend in Part III.

- Part III explains practical approaches to ensure your students' steady growth in comprehension. Chapters 6, 7, and 8 show you how to make sure everything you do is working to develop students' mental abilities before, during, and after reading.

And all along the way, we focus on the importance of motivating your students and developing their identities as readers, as well as your own.

We also include stories in every chapter, incorporate snippets of relevant research, and turn quickly to practical application. For example, we show you a simple way to hold your students accountable for independent reading in ways that won't tax your energy. We show you high-value writing activities that help students unpack the wide variety of sentences they encounter in texts. Our primary audience, as always, is you, the teacher, who works so hard to ensure every student is learning to read well and with confidence.

Doing all those things fuels students' reading growth until comprehension becomes every student's superpower, rather than their problem.

We show you how to help each student thrive as a reader. We argue for the value of curiosity and how to notice what your students need so they can build and sustain the genuine pleasure that bubbles up when one's curiosity is sparked through reading. And we show you what it can look like when a classroom—or a whole school—celebrates words, texts, and learning. Doing all those things fuels students' reading growth until comprehension becomes every student's superpower, rather than their problem.

We've been worrying—a lot—that essential aspects of reading other than foundational skills are being neglected in conversations around the science of reading. So, with this book, we reenter the conversation and broaden it. We lay out, in the same friendly manner of our first book, what else is crucial: comprehension.

Our Core Beliefs

Over the years, we've made mistakes that have informed our core beliefs. Those in turn have shaped our teaching of children, our teaching of teachers, and, now, this book.

We assure you, our own journey to solid outcomes for our students was uneven and downright rocky at times. "Know better, do better" applies to us as much as it does to any other practitioner. The parents of our students helped us toward success by forcing us to justify our decisions when they didn't understand them, especially when our school got the lowest reading scores in the city. We've learned—painfully—that failure is opportunity if we take the chance to do things differently.

We made plenty of mistakes, even when we were on the right track. Here are some of our whoppers:

- We didn't provide enough texts reflecting the full range of our students' identities, nor did we do enough to celebrate their cultures.
- Our students should not have been reading only fiction in literature groups.
- Despite learning much about the world from our curriculum, our students didn't read full-length books to study history and science. That was a missed opportunity.
- Though many of our students read books on their own, not all did. We never achieved the kind of high-volume independent reading we wanted for our students.

We've learned a lot since then, so we've folded what we've learned into this book, as we did with foundational-skills practices in our first book, *Know Better, Do Better: Teaching the Foundations So Every Child Can Read*.

Foster curiosity and wonder!

All Students Deserve Language-Rich Classrooms

Effective instruction for multilingual learners is fun and lively, rich in discussions and student exchanges. It places a high value on the spoken word. Further, there are many approaches to teaching multilingual learners that have universal application. The label "English learner" covers a lot of ground, from students who are new to English to those who are fluent in English. Of course, because students come from a diverse range of backgrounds and experiences, designing instruction for universal application is simply good design.

Students need to see themselves as valued and present in the books they're reading to develop a sense of self as readers.

Here's more proof of that. Julie Washington has been researching language and dialect for decades, considering those points and many other related ones for years. Her recent work with Mark Seidenberg (Washington & Seidenberg, 2021) makes clear that there's a lot of overlapping benefit to language-rich approaches for anyone who speaks a home language that differs from the one they are exposed to at school, as is the case for many Black children, Indigenous children, or any students being raised in non-mainstream regions of the country, such as Appalachia. We've always believed learning at school should be fun and student-oriented and when there's a compelling research base that proves its effectiveness, well, that's about as good as it gets.

Reading and Writing, Speaking and Listening, Must Fill the School Day

The other compelling reason we emphasize language-rich classrooms is because of the considerable overlap between spoken English and written English. To us, it's clear both forms of language should be leveraged to maximize all students' learning. We're not alone. According to Seidenberg and Borkenhagen (2020), "Reading depends on spoken language. A child doesn't re-learn a language when they learn to read; they link what they've learned from talking and listening to what they're learning about print." We want to make sure students are learning a lot from reading and writing, talking and listening, and doing a lot of it.

Students Must See Themselves and Others in the Literature They Read

Students need a variety of texts and topics in their reading diet. We often think about that as offering a variety of genres and text structures. But that's only part of it. The topics, authors, characters, settings, and ideas students encounter should vary widely, too. Students also need to see themselves as valued and present in the books they're reading to develop a sense of self as readers, an ingredient, we argue, that is crucial to the outcomes we're all looking for.

Furthermore, they need access to books with characters that look and live like them, but also with people, settings, and cultures that are unfamiliar to them. That's the right and equitable thing to do, so everyone has access to books with characters that look and live like them and everyone also gets to read about people, settings, and ways that are completely unfamiliar. But there's even more to this. When readers are familiar with a book's topic or setting, it's easier for them to make the crucial connections that lead to comprehension. You'll learn about that in Chapter 1: "The Role of Knowledge." Readers don't have to work as hard to make connections because they're swimming in familiar and comfortable waters. That's good because it builds confidence and is an important assist to comprehension. But reading for deep understanding is often hard work. In supportive ways, we need to provide all students with frequent opportunities for productive struggle. Otherwise, we won't build their reading muscles and capacity to hang in there when the going gets tough.

A Note on Teaching Multilingual Learners

In educational settings and in instructional materials, the needs of English language learners are often marginalized. We don't do that in this book. We weave in frequent modifications that support multilingual English learners—and everyone else—through a universal design approach to teaching ELA.

We're fans of "designing at the margins," the idea that when designing systems, accounting for the needs of the group(s) furthest away from the center of our attention will end up serving everyone better, and often in unexpected ways. That's definitely true when it comes to teaching multilingual learners (MLs). The language-rich practices we include help MLs learn to speak and understand what they read in English in order to thrive alongside their peers—while making learning more vibrant for all students. When we introduce such a practice, we call your attention to it with this blue symbol:

Foundational Skills Undergird Everything We Say, But They Aren't Our Focus

We were surprised by the positive reception of *Know Better, Do Better: Teaching the Foundations So Every Child Can Read.* A lot of teachers have told us that they found it friendly and helpful. They've told us it doesn't make them feel guilty for the things they didn't know. They've told us it laid the groundwork for learning about reading. And that's gratifying. We suspect their response was largely due to how forthright we were about overhauling a public school, and highlighting the mistakes we made. Between the two of us, we've worked in schools for more than 50 years. That's a lot of time to make mistakes!

But that book was only about one aspect of reading: foundational skills. Though we don't discuss those skills in this book, their importance is hovering in the background. When students haven't attained solid foundational skills, you can still build their comprehension and confidence, and we show you how. Foundational skills, essential as they are, are just part of the reading story. This book tells the rest of the story.

In Closing...

In Part I, we show you how to punch up students' knowledge of the world, vocabulary, and understanding of how words and sentences work—the essential building blocks of reading comprehension.

PART I
WHAT KIDS NEED TO KNOW TO COMPREHEND TEXTS

CHAPTER 1

The Role of Knowledge

Beginning in the fall of 1993, the Family Academy, the school we started in Harlem, transitioned from a balanced literacy approach to a structured literacy approach.[1] With the help of Marilyn Jager Adam's *Beginning to Read* (1991) and Tim Rasinski's pragmatic, widely available fluency work, we developed our own foundational-skills program. Students exiting second grade could read grade-level texts with fluency and verve, and most of them loved to read and be read to. But there were often gaps in their understanding of what they read. Standardized test results showed improvement, but lots of room for more—and we knew that before any results came back. Our students were reading better, but not as well as we knew they could.

"Boar Out There," a beautiful short story by Cynthia Rylant, helped us understand why. David was working with a group of our fourth graders, and it soon became clear that, though they

---

[1] This was long before those terms were in vogue, but that's what we did.

could answer questions about details and sequence of events and offer good insights about the girl in the story, they were fuzzy on the theme and even what kind of story it was. It soon became clear why. Early on, the story tells of a boar "that might have had a golden horn on his terrible head." (Rylant, 1988) In talking to the fourth graders about the story, and about their thinking while reading it, it became clear they weren't sure if a golden horn was a typical part of boar's anatomy. Because they didn't know the boar was a fictional creature, they also couldn't see how it was causing such disruptive fear. This wasn't an informational text, nor a science or social studies reading. It was a beautifully written allegory. Yet, that one piece of missing knowledge got in the way of the students' understanding—students who read fluently and were capable of understanding what they read. They knew they were confused but did not know why, or what to do about it.

That problem wasn't confined to texts like those used for instruction. The soul of the school was our well-stocked library, and every kid always had a book in hand. In the early years, the Goosebumps and Magic Tree House series were all the rage in upper elementary. Despite the simple language and predictable plots, the books contained a lot of references to attics, clipboards, the equator, manicured lawns, Norse and Egyptian gods, real estate offices, solar flares, on and on—things outside most of our students' knowledge.

The kids liked those books but it became clear when you hung out and asked them about what they were reading (a fun, valuable embedded diagnostic!) that unfamiliar references would sometimes throw them and prevent full comprehension.

Knowledge building is crucial—and rewarding!

We had overcome major hurdles in getting our foundational-skills instruction onto solid ground. Our students were reading fluently at grade level due to our inclusion of systematic phonics and fluency instruction, loads of practice, and the fact that, schoolwide, we were paying attention to developing Tier 2 vocabulary, as you'll read about in Chapter 2. But their lack of wide-ranging knowledge created a ceiling effect on their ability to make sense of what they were reading. And, apparently, we were on to something because the research before that time in the mid 1990s and since speaks to our concerns.

There's a Ton of Research Showing the Power of Knowledge

One of the most extensive reviews on the role of knowledge in reading was captured by Cervetti and Wright (2020) in the *Handbook of Reading Research, Volume V.* After sifting through decades of studies, they conclude, "Knowledge seems to have a greater impact on text comprehension than do general reading comprehension or decoding skills, and knowledge may help to compensate for lower levels of comprehension and decoding skill." This is a pretty stunning conclusion that doesn't only apply to nonfiction, but also fiction, as we saw with "Boar Out There."

> We had overcome major hurdles in getting our foundational-skills instruction onto solid ground.... But [students'] lack of wide-ranging knowledge created a ceiling effect on their ability to make sense of what they were reading.

In another review from Australia, Smith and his colleagues looked at 23 studies (Smith et al., 2021) that focused on the reading success of students ages 6 to 12 and noted, "We consistently found that higher levels of background knowledge enable children to better comprehend a text," and "This review highlights the importance of the systematic and sequential building of background knowledge for an increased ability to comprehend a range of texts in upper-primary school children." We could give you a lot more evidence, but we think you've got the point.

Those reviews helped us enormously in designing a program for the Family Academy that addressed knowledge building, along with the work of three major thinkers: E. D. Hirsch, Rudine Sims Bishop, and John Guthrie.

E. D. Hirsch and the Importance of Knowledge Building

We were familiar with E. D. Hirsch's work on knowledge building from flipping through his What Your Kindergartener [First Grader, Second Grader...] Needs to Know series of books. We found the lengthy topic lists overwhelming. We also noted that our own kids fell short of knowing many of those topics, even though we read aloud to them regularly and gave them lots of opportunities to expand their knowledge. But we got Hirsch's point: There is knowledge that educated people seem to gain almost by osmosis. And possessing it makes continuing to learn smoother for them. How do they acquire it? That question resonated with us because one of the core principles of the Family Academy was to open every possible door for our students so they could walk through any they chose. That principle drove a lot of our decisions. We didn't want any of our students excluded from anything because of things they didn't know. So, we needed to figure out how to make them knowledgeable people as a core part of their education.

When we bought all those books and dug into the topics Hirsch proposed, we realized some of the topics wouldn't work for us. A lot of the topics were too Eurocentric and didn't do justice to the rich histories, literary traditions, and stories of our students. We wanted them to know and take pride in their histories, traditions, and stories, while coming to know and appreciate other people's.

Rudine Sims Bishop and the Importance of Inclusive Reading Experiences

Rudine Sims Bishop's (1990) seminal research spells out the importance of students having different types of reading experiences. But it would be years before we learned of her perfect metaphor of children's literature serving as "mirrors, windows, and sliding glass doors"—of children seeing themselves and others in texts, and entering new worlds through texts. She named what we were striving for beautifully.

We wanted to drench our curriculum with reading experiences that would expose students to general knowledge that would assist them in their school and life journeys, as well as familiarize them with their own cultures' histories and contributions.

But what knowledge specifically? And where were we to find it, if not in Hirsch's books?

John Guthrie and the Importance of Topic-Focused Instruction

John Guthrie developed Concept-Oriented Reading Instruction (CORI) (Guthrie et al., 2009). CORI's power came from the fact that all instruction—everything students read and was read to them, and the focus of writing, discussions, art projects—revolved around one topic at a time.

Students in CORI consistently outperformed students in basal programs or balanced literacy programs on every measure Guthrie used, including student-motivation and standardized-reading assessments. Most importantly, the results CORI students enjoyed grew out of their classwork organically. The learning was rich, and it built knowledge students valued. There was no test prep or overemphasis on reading comprehension skills. Guthrie's work has informed our work, and we wish it were better known.

We hope by now we've made the case for the power of knowledge building in our educational system and its benefit for comprehension. We'll give cognitive scientist Dan Willingham the last word here. He notes that knowledge works like compound interest. It builds on itself powerfully, so the earlier we start to grow it, the better (Willingham, 2006).

The General Knowledge Curriculum (GKC)

With a gobsmacked Meredith looking on, David created the Family Academy's General Knowledge Curriculum (GKC).

He started by purchasing a recently published, expensive, and enormous book he'd learned about in his vocabulary research called *The Educator's Word Frequency Guide* (Zeno et al., 1995), which contained lists of frequently encountered words in the books most commonly read in U.S. schools, Grades 2–12. During the spring and early summer of 1995, David pored over that book nights and weekends, transposing the most frequently encountered words at each grade level onto numerous legal pads.

From there, David spent weeks staring at those lists until he saw patterns forming for the Tier 3 words that clustered themselves into broad content categories. He then took the 10 or so categories of highest-frequency words he saw at every grade level and used them to come up with topics for students to study, one grade below where they appeared most commonly in U.S. classroom texts. That way, our students would have encountered many of the words before they were likely to encounter them in grade-level text. For example, if large numbers of words related to biology showed up in lists for sixth grade, David would set *habitat* as a topic of study for fifth grade to smooth the path for our students in that grade.

Creating a Culture That Values Knowledge

When we started the Family Academy, we believed, and still do, that speaking, listening, reading, and writing should permeate the school day, along with tons of physical activity and hands-on learning opportunities. We didn't worry about blurring the lines between subjects. That meant teachers didn't have to stress about staying on schedule when a fascinating topic captured the students' imagination and consumed more of the day than planned.

We developed topics to ensure the depth and breadth of learning our students deserved. There were GKC units on topics such as the kingdoms of Central Africa, Mesoamerican art, Mexican poets, the history of the Caribbean, space, dinosaurs, weather, and influential Islamic mathematicians. The topics became the content of our social studies and science curricula, and we also folded topic reading into language arts activities throughout the day.

> Speaking, listening, reading, and writing should permeate the school day, along with tons of physical activity and hands-on learning opportunities.

We incorporated GKC topics into the culture of the school, as well as related vocabulary. We also expanded many of them from year to year. For example, the librarians set up displays of books connected to each topic for the kids who wanted even more information. Teachers plastered the hallways with artwork and student writing connected to the topic, and, whenever possible, parents and neighbors with related expertise came in to talk to classes.

And then there was "General Knowledge Jeopardy," which brought topics to life. For each grade, we made lists of straightforward questions inspired by the topics the students were studying, such as, "What were the rulers of Ancient Egypt called?"; "What are three West African Kingdoms you know?"; "What are the planets?"; and "Where do plants get their energy?" On the day of their turn at this much-anticipated event, one grade at a time would pour into the auditorium. Unlike real *Jeopardy*, the contestants rotated to give each student a chance to take the stage to answer questions over the course of the week. We awarded one point for each correct answer. It was a true competition. The kids wanted to win for their class, and so did the teachers! The most competitive teachers would occasionally contest answers, causing us to double-check and tiebreak if needed. It was a fun celebration of knowledge that we all looked forward to.

Students felt learning about the world at school was cool. They weren't doing it just to become better readers and score higher on the state assessments.

The Power of "Knowing Stuff"

We've seen how the value of "knowing stuff" plays out in classrooms we've visited.

- A fifth-grade class studying the NASA space program debated whether money should be spent on the program rather than on pressing needs in communities across the country, including their own. The discussion was focused and often heated. When the teacher complimented them, she also told them how rare it was for students their age to engage in this kind of debate, drawing the two sides together over the issue of "kids being disrespected!" And "all kids should be having debates like this!" These kids internalized a lot: Knowing about the world is interesting and important, and kids have a right to this knowledge.

- Two kindergarten students nearly came to blows over whether what they were watching crawl up a hallway wall was an "arachnid" or "an insect" (their word choices). David helped them settle the debate by gently halting the creature and counting its legs with them. They returned to their class and their "Bugs, Bugs, Bugs" unit pleased to share their experience. These kids were learning so much—that knowing about the world was fun, and that sharing new knowledge with peers was important.

- While studying Greek mythology, fourth graders made up a game inspired by Greek gods and goddesses to play at recess. In addition to learning that gaining knowledge can be a fun experience, they were exercising their minds, bodies, and creative muscles.

- A fifth-grade class containing a number of students who had recently settled in the United States was beginning a study of immigration, which included reading parts of the Universal Declaration of Human Rights. The planned lesson came to a halt when some students insisted on sharing their own refugee experiences. The other students were moved by those experiences and shocked to learn that kids they knew had lived through them. These students were learning about the world and that injustice was not as abstract and as far removed from their reality as they had thought. It reached right into their classrooms.

Knowing stuff had status with our kids. Your efforts will be more effective and enjoyable if students and parents see growing knowledge as a valued and celebrated part of school. We look forward to hearing what you already do, and what you devise if we've convinced you in these pages.

🌐 Learning about the world is for all students—students who are learning to speak English, monolingual English speakers struggling with grade-level text, and students reading effortlessly. Knowledge-building experiences are for everyone.

All students at every reading level can engage in learning about the world together. One teacher, holding back tears, said in a debrief, "It's *not* that my struggling readers are more involved than they ever were before; it's that they were more involved *than I ever thought they could be*." Because struggling readers have access to the same core text as everyone else, and to related text sets with books at a range of complexities, they knew what they were learning wasn't "dumbed down." Because they engaged in rich classroom discourse, they also knew they were a valuable part of their community of learning.

This dynamic learning also travels home. Kids who are learning exciting stuff want to talk about it. We've heard many stories from families of brisk dinner-table discussions about what their children were learning about.

And don't leave your creativity at home! Katherine Scotti's fourth graders in Baltimore City celebrate their learning at the end of each unit by displaying their projects, writing, and other work in the gym for parents, school administrators, and community members to browse. They also present what they learn in independent reading, explaining books in ways that go above and beyond what the core content covers. This rich ritual is Katherine's creation, not part of the program she was using. Furthermore, her students read in greater volume than her program calls for. Reading volume impacts knowledge building greatly, but it doesn't get the attention it deserves. It's also one of the thorniest challenges in elementary education. And it just happens to be the topic of the next section.

> Your efforts will be more effective and enjoyable if students and parents see growing knowledge as a valued and celebrated part of school.

What You Can Do to Build Your Students' Knowledge

Our experience shows and research confirms that two of the most effective practices to build knowledge are read-alouds in the early grades and the volume of reading thereafter.

Knowledge Building Through Read-Alouds

Here's a language-rich system for creating knowledge-building experiences through read-alouds. Though time can vary depending on how deeply you want to explore a topic, generally, these read-alouds should take about 15–20 minutes a day, 1–3 weeks per topic.

- Pick three to five books on a topic that you think students will respond to and/or are part of your curriculum (e.g., insects, bats, storms, food, vehicles). Decide which book will be your core text for the topic.

- Read aloud this core text first for pleasure, beginning to end, showing its pictures as you go. During this first reading, stop only if you think something left unexplained would mean students would be lost for the rest of the read-aloud.

- When you've finished the book, ask students if they have any questions, wonderings, or comments about the book, and capture them.

- Read the book a second time, this time focusing on addressing students' questions, wonderings, and comments (or your own) and see if your discussion leads to more questions, wonderings, and/or comments.

- Read the book a third time and discuss its concepts. For example, if the book is about insects and explains various body parts, be sure students understand each part, its function, and how it works with the other body parts. If the book is about weather and explains how differences in temperature cause winds or what a tornado is, explain those ideas. If the book is about life on a farm and explains how the nature of farm work changes with the seasons, explain that. You get the idea!

- Final read. Review some of the words that you feel need more time and attention, using your favorite vocabulary activities or the ones we suggest in Chapter 2. Of course, you can also drop in definitions to words your students don't know during any of the earlier reads. We explain "drop-in words" in Chapter 2.

- Last, address any lingering questions, wonderings, and/or comments. You can try to find answers online with students or, better yet, use the remaining books on the topic to explain and expand understandings.
- Now, take the other books you gathered on this topic and read them aloud just once, allowing as much time for discussion and making connections to prior learning as you can.

Be sure to add some of your own questions, wonderings, and comments; it will make a difference for your students.

Watch a discussion between David and Meredith and K–2 teachers about the power of knowledge-rich read-alouds.

Knowledge Building Through the Use of Text Sets

In a study that focused primarily on low-income PreK and kindergarten students, Neuman and Kaefer (2018) showed that reading a series of texts on various science topics during morning meetings helped students learn the concepts and the words in those texts, and develop expressive language. The results were especially marked amongst the students who were just starting to speak English.

Reading a series of texts on one topic also awakens and fuels curiosity. It's innately satisfying. It's why when kids get hooked on a topic such as dinosaurs, sports, superheroes, music, or horses, they usually want to read books on that topic. In essence, they're creating their own text sets. While every topic won't be equally appealing to every student, most kids will find themselves interested once they stick their toes in. Regardless, the learning—the new knowledge and the new words—will stick. Some research, in fact, shows that a "moderate" amount of knowledge kindles more interest in similar topics later on (Garner & Gillingham, 1991).

Carefully select set topics to make sure all students' interests and identities are represented.

By no means does what students read or have read to them have to be limited to informational texts. The text sets could include biographies or good stories connected to their topics, such as *Bats at the Beach* for bats, or *Mae Among the Stars* for astronauts and space exploration, or *Zonia's Rain Forest* for ecosystems.

We've also heard from many PreK and kindergarten teachers that combining rich interactive read-alouds with phonemic awareness or phonics activities has made their days more intellectually satisfying, as well as jet propelled their students' foundational skills and knowledge-building skills.

Knowledge Building Through Volume of Reading

Knowledge building certainly isn't limited to what you have time to read aloud to students. Students can and will build knowledge independently if they have access to a series of texts on a topic. The idea is the same for younger students. Students read a series of conceptually coherent texts on a topic. Ideally, they would start with texts at lower levels of complexity and then build up to texts (on the same topic) at grade-level complexity.

> "[A coherent sequence of texts not only] makes it possible for students to read and understand a complex text, but it also teaches the student that they must use the knowledge they have acquired from one text in understanding the next. By staying within a single coherent topic, the student has a better chance of learning that crucial lesson than if he were reading texts that jump from one topic to another."
>
> —Walter Kintsch

Sarah Lupo and her colleagues (2018) built upon this idea with an approach called "Quad Text Sets" for use with adolescent readers. It works equally well with upper-elementary students. First, the researchers chose a grade-level text on a specific topic, which of course could relate to what the students were studying in any class. Then they chose texts at lower levels of complexity, including ones that included graphics and videos that built content knowledge and motivation. They used a variety of familiar routines (e.g., provided vocabulary, built in robust opportunities for discussion, addressed text structure). But the big value and differential in Lupo and her colleagues' approach was their use of a variety of simpler texts, including excerpts from young adult books, nonfiction articles such as those from Scholastic magazines, videos, and even infomercials. All sorts of materials were employed and sequenced to grow students' knowledge and motivation to read complex grade-level material.

According to Lupo, teachers using the Quad Text Set approach reported that it "helped their students build relevant content knowledge," "identify themes of challenging texts," "increased the amount of time that students read," and "motivated students to read more challenging texts." Not bad!

When you're building your own text sets, remember to aim for simplicity and start off with a general introduction to the new topic. Don't let perfect be the enemy of good here! Think about when *you* need to build knowledge about something complex. For example, think about claiming expenses for student loans on your taxes. You'd welcome a bulleted list—a simple explanation to learn what's what. The elegance of the writing isn't what's important in knowledge building. It's the accessibility of the information. Simplicity is a virtue when you're first learning about something.

Another crucial point about a simple and plain explanation is that it's far more accessible to readers who aren't yet proficient, and fine for students who are, which means it's probably well suited for everyone in your class. Once they know a bit about the new topic, less proficient students are more likely to be able to handle longer readings that contain more details and complex sentences. That's one reason accumulating knowledge is so valuable for strengthening reading comprehension.

Research shows that readers, even those that are determined as weaker readers by reading assessments, perform as well or better on passages about topics they're familiar with than high-ability readers who are not familiar with those topics (Recht & Leslie, 1988; Schneider et al., 1989; Stahl et al., 1991).

So don't worry too much if the texts in your set aren't beautifully crafted, or if you find yourself explaining more than you'd like and spending a bit more time on simpler texts. Your students will still be learning about the world around them and about reading.

Need Texts? Check Out Chat Bot Tools!

We're excited by the various free chat bot tools that are emerging. You can order up a grade range and indicate information you'd like included about a topic, and, within seconds, the bot will give you a series of gradated texts. You need to check for accuracy and content before using the texts with students, but there's potential for a lot of labor saving. We played with a chat bot to create a text set on volcanoes for fourth graders. We requested a general short article about volcanoes, then a text on what causes volcanoes. Then we asked for a short text on how underwater volcanoes can form island chains (archipelagos). Within less than a minute, we had three articles we could refine and use with students.

Turning Up the Reading Volume

We've established the best way to learn about the world is to read, listen to, and discuss texts on topics about the world. Providing that access is essential. So take as a preface to this section the mantra of "by any means necessary."

We're often asked how much reading students need to do to develop troves of knowledge. Unfortunately, specific numbers are sometimes hard to come by when it comes to reading. So ask yourself:

- How much reading is enough to establish a strong knowledge base?
- How many times does a student have to see a word before its meaning goes into long-term memory?
- How many times does a student have to decode a word successfully before he or she can read it automatically and effortlessly?
- How many times must a student practice reading a text aloud to read it fluently?

You get the idea. We don't know for sure, but we do have some compelling evidence for how important this is. And if there's a must-read study we reference in this entire book, it's probably this one—Cunningham and Stanovich's 1998 study on volume of reading and its impact on children's reading outcomes. It's been cited over 1,800 times, so we're not the only ones who think it's important. Their findings are stunning.

- "Reading volume made a significant contribution to multiple measures of vocabulary, general knowledge, spelling, and verbal fluency even after reading comprehension ability and non-verbal ability had been partialed out." That means a larger volume of reading improved all of those measures for students *regardless of their current reading ability*.
- Volume of reading influenced vocabulary and knowledge measures even into old age. The researchers note, "Reading a lot can even help to compensate for the normally deleterious effects of aging."
- Finally, and perhaps most important, the study claims that out-of-school reading is likely a "more potent source" of reading volume than reading done in school.
- This study provides two important insights: First, volume of reading is incredibly important. Second, though we have no target number of words, pages, or books students need to read to reap benefits,

we know they need to read a lot, likely more than they're able to do during a typical school day as currently structured.

Cunningham and Stanovich's article, "What Reading Does for the Mind," influenced our own reading journey immensely. It influenced our work teaching, running schools, and working with schools, districts, and publishers. And in raising our own kids!

But in our experience—and we bet in yours, too—it's not easy to get most kids to read at home, and it seems to be getting harder by the year. Finding time in school is also a real challenge. But we need to keep trying. The stakes are too high not to.

How to Incorporate More Reading Into the Day

Students need stuff they can read independently, whether it's grade-level or not. Furthermore, if the texts they read are topically connected or on a topic students are studying in class, their vocabulary will grow more than it would with the same volume of topically unconnected texts (Cervetti et al., 2016; Landauer & Dumais, 1997). As their knowledge and vocabularies grow, students will be able to read increasingly complex texts. Though studies can't give us a quantity of pages or texts or words, they do give us a better understanding of how to increase the volume of reading, along with how important knowledge is.

> Students need stuff they can read independently, whether it's grade-level or not…. As their knowledge and vocabularies grow, [they] will be able to read increasingly complex texts.

To maximize knowledge about new topics, look for simple texts that convey ideas directly and connect them clearly. Keep in mind that students who require a lot of knowledge benefit from coherent texts, meaning the author took pains to connect ideas explicitly (Voss & Silfies, 1996; Best et al., 2006). No text is too simple. If the subject is central to learning goals, or catches the reader's interest, make a wider array of texts available to students who want them. They will!

David started his career teaching fifth grade in rural Wisconsin. The first unit in the science curriculum was about energy. Despite his own education, he knew nothing about energy. But he found the students' textbook super helpful in learning about it. Because the book was part of a grade-specific series, he read the chapters on energy in the books for earlier grades, which were even more helpful. To grow knowledge, no source is too simple. Reflect on that. If you need to learn something quickly, you need the simplest, clearest explanation. That goes for your students, too—until they get hooked on the topic.

On a related note, Willingham (2006) asserts that "not all knowledge needs to be detailed." He uses Benedict Arnold as an example, noting that children reading text about the Revolutionary War that refers to Benedict Arnold wouldn't need to learn details of his life, or the story of how he feuded with Alexander Hamilton. Knowing he was an important player in the War of Independence and then was a traitor is adequate. That means the texts you use to grow knowledge need to be treated differently than other texts. You don't test students on them or have students write time-intensive responses. But do be sure students are reading and gaining knowledge. We've come up with quick, fun ways to determine whether students have done that, which we call "lightweight student accountabilities." On the next page is an example of our favorite: "Rolling Knowledge Journal."

Learning about the world is fun!

KNOW BETTER, DO BETTER: COMPREHENSION

Rolling Knowledge Journal

Expert Pack: Earth's Precious Resource

1. Read each selection in the text set, one at a time.
2. After you read each selection, stop and think about new and important information you learned about the topic, and then write, draw, or list what you learned.
3. Write, draw, or list how the selection extends what you've learned from other resources you've read.

Download a blank copy of the "Rolling Knowledge Journal."

Selection	New and Important Information About the Topic	How Does This Selection Extend What I've Learned From Other Resources I've Read?
1. "For the World's Poor, Drinking Water Can Kill"	Lack of clean drinking water affects about 800 million people in the world.	
2. "Millions Lack Safe Water"	Lack of clean drinking water affects people in different places in different ways.	The maps show all the different places the 800 million people affected live; and the facts. Describes the many ways people are affected by the lack of clean water.
3. "The Water Cycle"	This tells how water evaporates, then precipitates from clouds to the earth, where it is stored as ground water until it evaporates again.	Describes how the water cycle works on Earth every day.
4. "Water, Water, Everywhere!"	There are many sources of water on Earth.	Even though water is everywhere, not all water can be used as clean water.
5. "Hydrology: The Study of Water"	This study provides basic information about the study of water.	This book explains the science behind water and how water affects history and the future.
6. "A Drop Around the World"	Water gets used over and over on Earth.	This story gives a lot of examples and pictures of how the water cycle matters to everyone and everything on Earth.
7. "Researchers Discover Huge Underground Water Reserve in Africa"	There is water underground, and researchers are trying to learn more about it.	Hydrologists study water. They can use their expertise to find out more about the underground water in Africa. Their research could help millions of people.
8. "What is Your Water Footprint?"	Makes me think about how much water I use in my life.	The website gave me ideas for how I can conserve water.

(Developed by Student Achievement Partners and licensed under CC 3.0, 2014)

The acquisition of knowledge should be our priority with volume of reading, not the quality of student work proving it or evidence that students have absorbed every detail.

Other Options to Increase the Volume of Reading

Teachers always have too much to do, so we don't want getting your students to read more to add to your workload.

OPTION 1: MAKE INDEPENDENT READING A PRIORITY.

Reading a lot in whatever form the text takes should become part of your culture. That can come about through a mix of encouragement and competition.

Mr. Morrisey, a fifth-grade teacher we say more about in the next chapter, is invested in making sure his students do a lot of reading on their own. He created a Google spreadsheet for students to keep track of their reading. They captured book titles and kept a tally of the total words they each read on their own through the year. He had students gleefully recording millions of words read, and reported it's been a terrific motivator. Classroom culture matters.

Book Log

Date	Title	Author	Genre	Rating (1–5)	Words Read
9/5	Who Was Ruth Bader Ginsburg?	Patricia Brennan Demuth	Nonfiction	5	7,580
9/7	Becoming RBG	Debby Levy	Nonfiction	5	17,122
9/10	The Lemonade Crime	Jacqueline Davies	Realistic Fiction	5	22,345
9/12	Blended	Sharon M. Draper	Realistic Fiction	5	49,971
9/12	Drama	Raina Telgemeier	Graphic Novel	4	8,466
9/13	Amulet: The Stonekeeper	Kazu Kibuishi	Graphic Novel	4	4,398
9/13	Amulet: The Stonekeeper's Curse	Kazu Kibuishi	Graphic Novel	5	6,673
9/14	Amulet: The Cloud Searchers	Kazu Kibuishi	Graphic Novel	5	6,801
9/16	Invisible Emmie	Terri Libenson	Realistic Fiction	5	11,939
9/16	Amulet: The Last Council	Kazu Kibuishi	Graphic Novel	3	7,103

Download a copy of the "Book Log."

Other teachers have taken their leveled book baskets and worked alongside students to reorganize them into topical book baskets. They then let students pursue their own interests by reading entire baskets worth of books on a given topic. This became a movement among teachers known as the "Book Basket Challenge." You can also use your school or public librarian to help bring connected titles into your room once your students have expressed areas of interest. And, of course, you can connect to any of the topics you're studying.

These are all variations on independent reading systems. The important difference with what we recommend is reading topically, with an emphasis on growing knowledge, and the idea of accountable student reading—real accountability, but kept lightweight for teachers. That way, students' focus stays on the content of what they're learning about.

OPTION 2: LET STUDENTS CHOOSE BOOKS BASED ON CURRENT, UPCOMING, OR PREVIOUS TOPICS YOU'RE COVERING.

It's important for students to have some level of choice in what they read. But for that to happen, the classroom library needs to be well stocked and well organized. So include books at a variety of complexity levels on topics you're teaching, plan to teach, or have taught.

Expect students to read a minimum of 15–20 minutes daily (in school or at home) from their chosen book. Use the lightweight accountabilities developed for the Text Set Project, such as the "Rolling Knowledge Journal" we showed you earlier.

Alternatively, have students make a short, informal presentation to the class from a generic framework you design. We like this approach because it spreads the knowledge across the class. We're big fans of public speaking and anything that activates oral language interactions.

Another possibility is to devote five minutes each day, say in morning meeting, and choose a few students at random to present for a couple of minutes what they learned in their reading the night before.

OPTION 3: LET STUDENTS PICK THEIR OWN BOOKS, NARRATIVE OR INFORMATIONAL, DRIVEN BY THEIR INTERESTS.

The difference here is students choose according to whatever they like, regardless of current, previous, or future topics. So the accountability needs to be slightly different. We'd anticipate that many students would choose to read narrative fiction for their free-choice reading. Of course, fiction teaches us about the world just as informational text does. We'd suggest a simple tracking chart like this:

Free-Choice Reading Tracker

Book Title: Make Way for Dyamonde Daniel	Read by: Sara

For the chapter or pages you read, record your thoughts briefly in one of the last two boxes. You don't have to fill out both.

Date	Chapter/ Pages Read	What did you learn about people or the world?	What was a highlight of this reading?
2/2	Intro	This book is about 2 new kids, Dyamonde and Free who are in the same 3rd-grade class.	
2/3	1–24	Dyamonde is really smart and good at math. Free is really grumpy and quiet and mean. They're both new and don't have any friends. Free came from Detroit.	
2/5	25–42		Dyamonde wonders what's wrong with Free. Her teacher tells her to ask but he won't answer. She's stubborn and keeps trying and gets after him for being mean to littler kids.
2/6	43–52	The 2 kids get to know each other. They both had to move and didn't want to. They're neighbors! They get to be friends. Free is a good reader and starts to act better in class now that he has a friend.	
2/7	53–74		How the 2 kids become nice and start hanging out! They're different in some ways but they seem to be more alike once they get to know each other.

Download a copy of the "Free-Choice Reading Tracker."

Given the difficulty of getting all students to read at home, one key guiding principle when it comes to achieving volume of reading is that classroom lessons shouldn't depend on students doing a ton of reading outside of class. We're not talking about regular homework for reinforcing class learning, even though we know getting homework done is a perennial classroom-management challenge! We're talking about achieving additional reading.

The next day's work shouldn't depend on it. Nonetheless, getting students to read more is something worth fighting for.

Consider sending voicemail reminders of evening reading to caregivers (and/or directly to older students) that arrive at a preselected time in the late afternoon or early evening. Teachers have told us that this can make a huge difference and, of course, could be used for any of the suggestions we've made that would benefit from family involvement.

The driving idea behind all of these is to maximize reading at home without counting on this for the next day's work.

In Closing, Remember...

- Abundant findings from educational and cognitive science research attests to the essential role of knowledge.
- Knowledge building can be accomplished through read-alouds. In later grades, it can be accomplished through independent reading of texts that are easy to read and not necessarily of high literary quality.
- Reading a series of texts on a topic grows more knowledge than series of texts on different topics.
- Encouraging a love of knowledge motivates students to acquire it.
- By having all students learn the same topics and reading similar texts, you motivate weaker readers.
- The more texts students read, the more their knowledge grows.

Building knowledge sits at an interesting intersection in reading comprehension. Readers need to know something about references authors make or they'll struggle to understand. You'll learn much more about that in Chapter 5. On the other hand, readers can learn many new things from what they're reading. They can learn the meaning of words from context more easily if they possess a good deal of topic knowledge about what they're reading.

It's time to turn our attention to vocabulary and its importance to comprehension.

CHAPTER 2

Vocabulary: Meaningful Words

Words were everywhere, used in all kinds of ways, at the Family Academy. Take for example, the hall pass, a school-wide practice. Each week, our teachers would put five words on a binder ring. When students needed to leave the classroom to, for example, use the restroom, they would take the words with them and be prepared to discuss them with anyone they passed in the hallway.

It wasn't uncommon to see students dancing from foot to foot as they answered David's queries regarding their knowledge of the words on their hall pass. More than once, teachers had to remind David to check with children if they were returning from the bathroom or heading there

and to please postpone the conversations if they hadn't gotten there yet. They also had to reassure students that it was fine to tell David they were on an *urgent* mission, if that was the case.

Each week, the teachers would retire words from their rings and post them on the walls of the building's main hallway, a giant train of words that eventually wrapped throughout the school. Students often lingered in the hallway to hunt down words they'd studied.

Hallway-pass words were just some of the words we celebrated and studied across subject areas. More than one teacher followed fourth-grade teacher Ms. Lange's practice of temporarily banning the use of Tier 1 words, such as *good*, *bad*, *glad*, and *sad* to describe events and feelings. Instead, the teachers challenged students to use more precise words to convey whatever they *really* meant. We'd frequently hear exotic adjectives, verbs, and nouns flying around the playground and hallways.

Though we didn't know it then, the relationship between robust vocabularies and strong reading comprehension had been explored for decades, starting in 1925 with Guy Montrose Whipple's Report of the National Committee on Reading.

Jeannie Chall, perhaps the most universally revered reading researcher in history, once postulated that vocabulary is so strongly correlated with reading comprehension that there is no real need for separate comprehension assessments if children demonstrate abundant word knowledge (Chall & Jacobs, 2003).

What we did know from our observations, as well as the research David was rapidly digesting, was that reading has a lot to do with words! How many words our students were comfortable using and could recognize—heck, how well they liked words and found them a source of pleasure—had a palpable impact on their reading success. So did using those words when they spoke and wrote, until they were no longer new and unusual, but a part of them. Last but not at all least, our teachers also needed to develop a curiosity about and interest in exploring words, alongside their students.

Tiers of Vocabulary

In 2002, Isabel Beck and Margaret McKeown introduced the useful notion of dividing up all English words into three tiers as a way to set priorities for vocabulary instruction (Beck et al., 2013).

Tier 1 Words

In their scheme, Tier 1 words are basic words that children generally learn through daily interactions, such as *breakfast*, *fun*, *spoon*, *cat*, and *soup*. Children won't learn them at the same rate, but most children, once exposed to spoken English regularly, will learn them sooner or later. These words tend to be highly concrete and easy to visualize—the simplest word for communicating what something means.

Tier 2 Words

Tier 2 words, such as *variety*, *particular*, *specifically*, and *including*, are sometimes used in daily interactions, but are much more likely to show up in texts. In fact, they play a significant role in making texts more complex as students move up the grade levels. They're important. Why? For one thing, they show up all the time in all sorts of texts—informational texts and literary texts, and help to make those texts nuanced. Because they aren't subject specific, they aren't the focus of any one subject area. That's a danger to students' learning them because they are nobody's direct responsibility the way Tier 3 (content words) are. Tier 2 words and the work they do to contribute meaning must not be neglected. Directly attending to them in instruction ensures students' awareness of them and gives kids a chance to think about their meaning and specific role in the text (Snow, 2010; Adams, 2009).

This avid reader is the child of one of our Family Academy students.

To get a sense of how important Tier 2 words are, try to reread the opening paragraphs of this section with those words missing.

Stripping Tier 2 words from a text makes it clear what they contribute to meaning. Not knowing just a few of these words can wipe out understanding for readers. It can also reduce how much students learn about any topic as Tier 2 words support learning about the concepts they help describe.

In 2002, Isabel Beck and Margaret McKeown _____ the _____ _____ of _____ up all English words into three _____ as a way to set _____ for vocabulary instruction (Beck et al., 2013). In their _____, _____ 1 words are _____ words that children generally learn through _____ _____, such as *breakfast*, *fun*, *spoon*, *cat*, and *soup*. Children won't learn them at the same _____, but most children, once _____ to spoken English _____, will learn them sooner or later. These words _____ to be _____ _____ and easy to _____.

Tier 3 Words

Tier 3 words, also known as domain vocabulary, tend to belong to one subject area—words such as *erosion*, *colonial*, *circumference*, and *photosynthesis*. So students tend to encounter them in subjects other than ELA (*erosion* in earth science, *colonial* in history, *circumference* in math, *photosynthesis* in life science). Because they help to explain the core concepts of those domains, we tend to take good care to introduce and discuss Tier 3 words as they come up in learning.

The stakes are high when it comes to helping students build robust stores of words—especially words they aren't likely to be able to figure out on their own when they encounter them in text. The truth is, students aren't impacted equally by how much attention we pay (or don't pay) to developing strong vocabulary practices in school. That's because their exposure to words varies outside of school. Lily Wong Fillmore, a linguist who's had a tremendous influence on teaching multilingual learners, often says nobody is a native speaker of academic English, but children from formally educated families tend to learn much of it at home through discussion, having their media monitored, and, especially, being read to. Many other researchers have found the same thing (Cunningham & Stanovich, 1998; Stanovich, 1986). Clearly, helping all students grow their vocabulary matters, and we'll show you how to do that later in this chapter.

Vocabulary Breadth and Depth— Developing Both Is Crucial

There are two elements of vocabulary: breadth and depth. Breadth means the total number of words you know—words you have a general sense of, or know the most common meaning of. So, if you know the word *common* means ordinary, you're probably good to go when you see it while reading. The other way to know vocabulary is to know words more deeply—or to know them in depth.

Depth means how well you know a word. Knowing the word *common* in depth means you know it as an adjective that means shared and as a noun that means a place that a whole community can use (as in a New England town common or a building's common room). You probably know the expression "in common" (as in "We have a lot of things in common, that's why we're good friends"). Going back to the meaning of *common* as ordinary, you likely know that *common* is the opposite of unusual and rare, its antonyms. You might even know that in England, the word *commoner* means someone who is ordinary, who isn't in the noble class (and that those English commoners are represented in Parliament by the House of Commons). You might even know the adjective form can be used in a mean way: so ordinary, it's lacking class or is cheap, as in, "The way she dresses makes her look common." You probably know *common* is related to *communal* and *community*, both building off the shared sense of *common*. In short, as a mature reader, you know a lot about the word *common*, and when you see it, you know which sense of meaning is in play in that situation. That deeper knowledge of the word *common* helps you to understand the nuances of sentences that contain it, and to grasp the author's themes and concerns.

Depth and breadth of vocabulary are correlated with comprehension (Binder et al., 2017), and support different elements of comprehension (Cain & Oakhill, 2014; Ouellette, 2006).

Vocabulary Breadth Supports Comprehension

Vocabulary breadth supports comprehension in two important ways.

1. Using context clues to figure out the meaning of unknown words makes sense, but students can only use context if they know the meaning of the words that create the context of that unknown word. That requires breadth of vocabulary (*and* knowledge, by the way). Having a broad working vocabulary (greater breadth) provides an important comfort level with text—a reader's sense that he or she belongs in books like these because he or she recognizes the majority of its words. That confidence boost is invaluable to reading success.

2. Students' oral vocabulary plays a key role in effortless and automatic decoding. And effortless and automatic decoding is the foundation for fluent reading, which comprehension rests upon. It all stacks on itself. Here's how that works. A student sees a word. If the student knows that word, even just orally, he or she can fire up its meaning and correct pronunciation while decoding it accurately. That means the word's meaning and proper pronunciation are more likely to be cemented. The student has successfully read it and can move on. Again, this can happen with words the young reader has never seen before, but has heard. In sum, breadth of vocabulary supports decoding and word recognition, an aspect of the science of reading that doesn't get the attention it merits.

Take *flexible*, a word from our school's third-grade vocabulary-ring hall pass. When the kids were discussing the word, Shanee said her grandmother always told her she was as flexible as a pipe cleaner! She'd never seen the word written before she saw the hall pass, but her grandmother's words helped Shanee and her classmates understand what *flexible* meant and how to pronounce it. When the class later read a story by Misty Copeland, the principal ballerina at the American Ballet Theatre, about how she'd fallen in love with ballet, they recognized and could read the word *flexible*, thanks to Shanee and their vocabulary-ring hall pass.

Now that *flexible* has been encountered in print, its phonic pattern, spelling, *and* meaning are more firmly cemented. That's known as "orthographic mapping," and it happens with each successful encounter of a word. This is what helps readers recognize words effortlessly (Ehri, 2014, 2023; Ouellette, 2006).

How You Can Help Students Develop Vocabulary Breadth

You just read about this in the knowledge chapter, so this is a lightning review. Vocabulary grows by reading a lot—in other words, by students' volume of reading. Makes sense, right? If students are reading a lot of text (or hearing a lot of text read to them), they're encountering lots and lots of words.

That's how children grow a large vocabulary, so they need us to create those conditions in our classrooms. There's important research about how that volume of reading should be connected that we've already covered in Chapter 1. Again, as a quick reminder: clustering that volume of reading on one topic for a period of time (long enough to read several things about it) builds knowledge of that topic while growing vocabulary way faster than skipping from topic to topic and reading randomly (Cervetti et al., 2016; Landauer & Dumais, 1997). This is true for children as young as early preschool, when the words they are taught were clustered into networks organized by concept and topic (Hadley et al., 2019; Neuman et al., 2011).

Why is reading within a topic so powerful? Think about it. Reading about a topic for a while takes you from novice to expert (or at least apprentice). Remember the importance of Tier 2 and Tier 3 words? They come into play here. When you're learning about a topic by reading informational text, the words that name important concepts are usually introduced and defined well by the author. Those words are, in fact, the concepts that underlie the topic.

David's Favorite Example of Developing Breadth

David was observing third graders immersed in an ELA curriculum that he had helped develop, organized by content-areas topics such as pollinators, human rights, and marine life. On the day David was observing, the students were reading a passage about dolphins for the first time, as part of their unit on marine life: "The scientists saw the dolphins ascend to the surface. They also were seen descending in groups." In the discussion that followed, the teacher never defined *ascended, surface,* or *descending* for the class. But it was clear from the students' comments that they had had a good idea why the dolphins were doing those things. So they could *infer* what those three sophisticated Tier 2 words meant. Why? Because they already knew dolphins were mammals with lungs, not fish with gills. That meant they needed to come up to breathe oxygen from the air. So to *ascend* must mean to come up. They also knew sea mammals eat things that live in the ocean. So they knew dolphins would likely go down, or *descend*, to feed. What's the *surface*? The plane between the air and the water, where the dolphins could go to fill their lungs with oxygen. Even though the teacher didn't explain any of the words, the students could define them based on topic knowledge they'd gained.

You can't fully understand plants without understanding *photosynthesis*, and you can't fully understand representative government without understanding *legislature*. So authors tend to go to great lengths to explain those words, and often repeat them. While a reader is immersed in that text, he or she is learning those concepts and the words that name them (lots of Tier 3 words and some of the Tier 2 words that qualify them). He or she is also becoming more knowledgeable about the topic as he or she reads. That means *lots* in the reading becomes familiar—providing context clues for whatever words are unfamiliar, many of which are Tier 2 words.

So reading volume, which we discussed in Chapter 1, is not only the best way to grow knowledge, but also to grow the breadth of Tier 2 vocabulary. Everything in reading bleeds into everything else. We can't afford not to capitalize on that synergy—growing vocabulary and growing knowledge are essential to deepening reading comprehension. Doing both together strengthens each. It also saves time and increases joy, both precious commodities.

> Everything in reading bleeds into everything else. We can't afford not to capitalize on that synergy—growing vocabulary and growing knowledge are essential to deepening reading comprehension.

Vocabulary Depth Supports Comprehension

The more students know about words, the stronger readers they are (Perfetti, 2007; Perfetti & Stafura, 2014). In addition to the depth and breadth of word awareness we already know about, there are other factors that, if known, can help to cement a word in a student's brain for keeps.

Those are a word's:

- Orthography (how a word is spelled)
- Phonology (how it's pronounced)
- Part of speech in its current context (the work it's doing in the sentence)
- Morphology (the word's meaningful parts)
- Etymology (the word's origin story)

Knowing some of those things about words contributes greatly to how nuanced the reader's understanding can be—how deep his or her comprehension can be. It's so essential. We look at morphology and etymology in depth in Chapter 3.

Cultivating the Habit of Paying Attention to Words

Important as it is, the habit of paying attention to words—of giving students opportunities to find particular words fascinating—isn't cultivated often enough in classrooms. We need to correct that. Creating a culture that invites your students to explore the English language, to make connections between words, and to have "aha!" moments, is essential.

Meredith was fortunate to have this culture at home, growing up. The youngest of seven children, she had a mother who kept a treasured oversized dictionary near where her large brood ate its meals. When a word came up in conversation that intrigued her, Meredith's mom would jump up and exclaim, "Seize the opportunity for the further acquisition of valuable knowledge!" She would then go over to the dictionary and read to Meredith and her siblings about the word. Talk about developing vocabulary breadth (and depth)! That was it in a nutshell. That well-worn *Webster's Unabridged Dictionary* lives in our study to this day, still open on its antique bookstand.

How You Can Help Students Develop Vocabulary Depth

As we just read, the more alert readers are to the nuances of words in a text, the deeper their comprehension of that text will be (Perfetti, 2007; Perfetti & Stafura, 2014). This comes from developing a curiosity about words and the work those words are doing to convey meaning. Developing this curiosity will do a lot to develop deep word knowledge.

You can cultivate the habit of caring about and learning to examine words by directly teaching words—through providing regular opportunities that allow for students to dive into and deeply investigate a select number of words. This can and should start ideally in preschool, and definitely in kindergarten. Some students get lots of these opportunities at home. That exposure shows up as examples of opportunity gaps between students with deep knowledge of words and students who haven't gotten to learn as much about the kinds of words used in books and in school. Schools must create conditions for *all* students to develop deep knowledge about words.

What exactly does "directly teaching words" mean? It means stopping to discuss an interesting word while you're engaged in reading a text with your students. This is essential. Stopping to discuss a word and why the author used it not only helps students learn the meaning of words, but also gives them time to think about them and see what a given word is doing in that context, and ponder how it might be different in another context. From there, have students play around with them using word games, puzzles, riddles, and anything else that supports deep interactions with words, word parts, and word origins.

Mr. Morrisey is a longtime fifth-grade teacher in Western New York who has been studying how to improve reading outcomes for elementary students for decades. A self-proclaimed "word nerd," he has created the conditions for all his fifth graders to become "word conscious" (aware of words) as a large part of his classroom culture. None of what he describes takes much time to stop and do.

Activities to Deepen Depth and Breadth

- Display words that students have studied on a classroom wall. During transitions, randomly select a word and ask a student to use it in a sentence or come up with a synonym or antonym for it, or give one or more of the word's meanings.

- Have students maintain a journal entitled "Words We Know a Lot About." During vocabulary study or morning meeting, have them suggest words to add to the journal and explain why. If you and other students agree with the suggestion, ask the student who made it to research the word and teach what he or she discovered about it to the class.

Words We Know a Lot About

Name: Antonio

Title of Book/Article: The Birchbark House by Louise Erdrich

Page	Word	Context (sentence it's in)	Meaning	Synonym	Antonym
19	isolated	Although she lived in town, Old Tallow was so isolated by the force and strangeness of her personality that she could have been surrounded by a huge dark forest.	Cut off, unable to connect with others	alone	surrounded
21	warily	Omakayas approached Tallow's cabin warily because of the dogs.	Very carefully, watching carefully	cautiously	carelessly
22	abrupt	"You want the scissors!" Her voice was abrupt but not unkind.	Sudden and brief	Curt, rough	slow
24	translucent	It came out beautifully, creamy-golden, translucent and grainy-dark.	Almost see-through (light passes through)	See-through	Cloudy, solid

Download a blank copy of a "Words We Know a Lot About" journal page.

Mr. Morrisey's Routines for Developing Vocabulary Depth

Here are a few of the many routines Mr. Morrisey incorporates.

- Uses Tier 2 words in place of ordinary words (e.g., "We're going to *reconvene* after lunch." and "Please *commence* cleaning up.")
- Periodically creates a continuum of words to teach students their nuances in meaning.

Here is his continuum of the word *change*: adjust → vary → alter → modify → amend → substitute → exchange → convert → transform → revolutionize

And here is his continuum of the phrase "bad smells": mildly unpleasant→ unpleasant→ offensive→ foul→ noxious→ putrid→ rancid

Mr. Morrisey reported that after sharing that last continuum of smelly words with fifth graders recently, one of his students farted during class. Without skipping a beat, the student next to him said, "Well, that is somewhere between putrid and rancid." It was a "word nerd" bonding moment for him and his students! He uses this activity to review science or social studies content, while creating a competition over who can use newly learned academic vocabulary accurately and frequently. He had recently introduced these words: *crucial, vital, essential, integral, manifest, exasperated, belligerent, devour, consume, significant, procure, unique, unified,* and *sustain.* From there, he challenged students to use them in their content writing for the week. Here are some examples of student writing from a science unit on plants:

- "Plants not only are crucial, vital, essential, and integral to life, they also manifest glucose for everything on earth to consume."

- "I become exasperated and belligerent when forced to devour and consume fruits and vegetables by my parents."
- "Some plants are significantly hard to procure due to some having a paltry amount of seeds."
- "The plant had a unique feature of making the leaves sticky to catch its helpless prey."
- "The two groups unified to make sure the beautiful garden will be sustained forever."
- "Plants are unique and also vital for oxygen and food."

This fabulous fifth-grade teacher shared more terrific examples with us, but you get the idea.

 Mr. Morrisey went on to say this about one girl in his class who had been speaking English for just three years:

"One day in math she said to my teaching partner, 'Mrs. H. I'm exasperated right now.' She was frustrated because she was struggling with multiplying decimals. On the same day she learned the word *delicate* and mentioned in front of the class, 'It is like fragile. They are things that can be easily broken.' It is cool when all students get into learning new words."

Spending time investigating vocabulary in depth, the way Mr. Morrisey does, makes students more aware of words and the varied work they do (Beck et al., 2003, 2013).

Once he started to notice academic vocabulary in texts and realize what he could do with it in the moment, he started to see those opportunities everywhere. When we spoke with him, his fifth-grade group had hit a midyear tipping point where *all students* were curious about words. They would connect new words to ones they'd learned earlier, and started to spot the morphemes they knew.

Developing breadth of vocabulary does require a commitment of time and resources. If your instructional materials include regular work with vocabulary that aligns with the principles outlined below, well, that's good news. If not, and you're not in a position to get a stand-alone vocabulary series for your students, how do you decide what words are worth that kind of time and attention? And if you are using an ELA program, how do you know if the words selected for deep study are well selected? And what the heck do you do with words you encounter in texts that many of your students don't know but *aren't* that valuable in the scheme of things?

Well, there are rock-solid answers to those questions, thanks to two great vocabulary researchers, Freddy Hiebert and Andrew Biemiller. Both have done a lot of important work in vocabulary and its connection to comprehension. Here are Freddy Hiebert's (2009) three criteria for choosing words for more involved work:

1. Words that are needed to fully comprehend the text
2. Words that are likely to appear in future texts from any discipline
3. Words that are part of a word family (or semantic network)

The first criterion holds, whether a word is likely to appear in future texts. We don't ever want students reading stuff they don't understand. So go ahead and define words that ensure comprehension, and keep moving. This epiphany, that we can quickly add new words to students' lexicons, is part of Andrew Biemiller's genius. He dubbed these "drop-in words" (Biemiller, 2010).

There are many times you can easily "drop in" definitions in this manner, which will grow your students' vocabulary. So you should do it regularly.

Four-Star Vocabulary Programs

There are two excellent stand-alone vocabulary programs we'd use if we were teaching now. One is WORD (Words Open Reading Doors), developed by vocabulary expert Elfrieda "Freddy" Hiebert. The other is *Wordly Wise 3000*.

Over time, this will get easier. Before you know it, you won't be able to look away from these opportunities! The criteria for good candidates for drop-in definitions are:

1. How concrete the words are. The more concrete, the easier to explain quickly.

2. Whether the words are synonyms for ideas and concepts students already know. Familiar words make great drop-ins.

Here are some examples.

New Tier 2 Word	Familiar Synonym
magnificent	great, wonderful
gargantuan	really big (like a blue whale)
extraordinary	unusual or special
gregarious	very friendly, the opposite of shy

Meredith's Favorite Example of Developing Breadth

Meredith had taken over a reading group for a teacher on extended leave. The students were reading *The Cay* by Theodore Taylor. They all *hated* the book and weren't shy about saying so. When Meredith asked why, they said they didn't understand why the two main characters, a snotty young boy and a blind elderly man who didn't like each other at all, didn't just part ways. The only exciting event as far as the students were concerned, was the torpedoing that had shipwrecked the protagonists and *that* happened almost immediately in the story. After that, the characters' rocky relationship and the adversity they face *were* the story. Not understanding what glued them together (their setting) made the whole story seem ridiculous to the group.

None of the students knew the significance of the title because they didn't know what a cay was (neither did Meredith until she looked it up). The teacher who started the book with them had missed the importance of revealing it. When we looked it up together and realized a *cay* (pronounced "key") is a small island made of a coral reef, and that this book was based on a real incident that happened near Curaçao during World War II, it made sense to them that these sole inhabitants of their cay were stuck with, and indeed, badly needed each other.

Cay is an example of what Andrew Biemiller (2010) calls a "drop-in word." This is a word that should be quickly explained in the moment of encounter without any further embellishment. These words are not candidates for deep analysis or morphological exploration. They don't need (or warrant) that kind of time. But they are crucial to understanding the text where they're encountered. Meredith's inherited reading group probably would have liked *The Cay* much more if they'd known from the beginning what the heck a cay was!

Hiebert's other two criteria for choosing words serve as useful guideposts. A quick reminder: these are words that are likely to show up as students move up the grades, and words that have a lot of semantic "relatives." Learning them will help students learn about many related others.

Once you start to have a sense of what constitutes a high-value word for your students, you need to develop a repertoire of activities to explore the words you select. A great way to do that is to get a group of teachers together to read and work through the guidance and exercises David developed called "Vocabulary and the Common Core." Scan the QR code to the right to access it. We offer a few other great activities in the resources section, starting on page 151.

Download a copy of "Vocabulary and the Common Core."

In the meantime, here are the criteria from Beck, McKeown, and Kucan's *Creating Robust Vocabulary* (2008) that must be considered for vocabulary instruction to improve comprehension:

- Multiple encounters with a new word
- Both definitional and contextual information
- Engagement of students in deep, active processing (using the word for themselves, playing with the word) (p. 4).

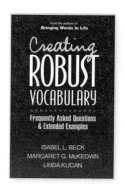

For vocabulary knowledge to be deep and rich, words need to be taught in energetic ways that encourage students to think about what they are learning. That's what the balance of this chapter is all about.

Engage Students in Word Learning

In general, when *students* are the ones expending the energy (meaning they're doing the processing work), they're learning. We teachers tend to talk too much. Students need to engage in discussions on words they're lingering on, use those words in their writing, get excited about them, and tell each other about words that share cognates from their home languages. We need to set the conditions for all that to happen and then give the room to do it; nothing elaborate. It should feel supportive and useful to everyone.

Here's an example.

Meredith loved William Steig's *Amos & Boris* as much as her kindergarteners did. It was often requested as their read-aloud book. The students were

discussing how unlikely the friendship between the mouse and the whale was and Meredith asked the students how they knew that Amos and Boris were good friends. Although they were certain, they had a hard time figuring out *how* they knew. Parish brought up the page where the characters say their goodbyes, and Boris pointed out, "they could be friends forever even if they couldn't be together," which helped some. Tomonia remembered that we'd talked about them having a "deep admiration for one another" and said she wasn't sure, but thought that was part of them being friends. She also commented that she still wasn't sure what *admiration* meant. There were lots of head nods to her comments, though a few of the students who spoke Spanish at home knew the verb *admirar* meant to respect someone. So we decided to explore what *admiration* meant. The kids organized themselves into groups based on the character they liked best. Then Meredith asked members of each group to share what they thought was most wonderful about their character, while our magnificent paraprofessional listed their responses on chart paper. They took lots of phrases straight from Steig, such as "deep purpose" and "full of wonder" as *admirable* traits. It was clear the students had a strong sense of these two lovable characters and their many positive qualities. We came back together to compare lists and agreed both characters had lots of good qualities. We went to Wordsmyth Word Explorer Children's Dictionary online and typed in *admire*. Meredith read much of the entry:

> **Definition 1:** to have a high opinion of; respect.
> *I admire my dad because he works hard, but he also takes time to be with us kids.*
> similar words: *appreciate, respect*
>
> **Definition 2:** to look at with delight, wonder, and approval.
> *Everyone was admiring my new bike.* similar word: *like*[2]

[2] She shortened these definitions because a few similar words at a time is all that is reasonable.

She then asked the students to do a turn-and-talk to process what they now understood *admiration* to mean. They leaned into the ideas of respect and enjoyment, and the class agreed that fit what Amos and Boris felt for each other. They decided that close friends probably should respect and enjoy each other most of the time, like Amos and Boris. This whole exploration took about 12 minutes, but the idea that questions have answers and words have valuable information to impart felt more than worth it.

This story is also the tale of a comprehension lesson. After all, this is a group of five- and six-year-olds using a text to determine what they believe are the qualities that make a close friendship. Thinking hard about ideas through studying sections of a text (here examining what the specific words in the text convey) was essentially examining the primary theme of this book. So we ask you: Was this a comprehension lesson or a vocabulary lesson? The great beauty and power of reading is that it clearly was both. And so it goes. In so many ways and so many times, the best lessons are multidimensional in just that way. All we need are great texts and great kids and teachers who are willing to be curious investigators together.

> The best lessons are multidimensional.... All we need are great texts and great kids and teachers who are willing to be curious investigators together.

A word here about writing and its relationship to building strong readers. Using newly learned words in their writing helps students cement their sense of what the word means and how it belongs in context. And just as you can see if early readers know a word's phonic pattern by how they're spelling it, you can see if your students understand a word by how they're using it in a sentence. Deep learning and quick diagnostic assessment in one healthy interaction—that's a good payoff. It also goes to the heart of engaging students in deep, active processing that Beck, McKeown, and Kucan talk about in *Creating Robust Vocabulary* (2008). We'll dive into the interaction between writing and reading more in Chapter 8.

There's no doubt knowing what's what in vocabulary instruction can be daunting: when to stop and teach a word quickly in context, when to prepare students in advance by preteaching words they'll encounter in a text, and when to teach words intensively.

We hope having some research-based criteria and practical examples will help you either do this for yourself or validate the selections made by the makers of the instructional materials you're using.

In Closing, Remember...

- One hundred years of research attests to the importance of vocabulary knowledge to proficient reading.
- By far, students encounter Tier 2 most frequently in the texts they read, which they need to understand Tier 3 words they encounter.
- Vocabulary breadth is the number of words for which a reader knows the most common meanings. It's best grown by reading a series of texts on a topic.
- Vocabulary depth is how much a reader knows about a word. It's best grown through close reading and developing a classroom and school culture that values and wonders about words.

Breadth and depth have a lot of synergy. If students develop curiosity about words, they are more likely to notice words they're not sure of when they encounter them while reading and stop to try to figure out their meaning (Beck et al., 2013). The more they do that, the more breadth of vocabulary they'll acquire. Once they start studying words in depth, they'll experience the payoff of coming *to know* words deeply and seeing connections among them. As students come to know words, they'll be able to figure out unknown ones more easily in context.

Synergies like that exist all across reading. Understanding them and taking advantage of them fuel students' proficiency. To add to that understanding, we move next to morphology and etymology, and what teaching them can do to help students come to know words deeply.

Morphology and Etymology: The Structure and Origin of Words

Morphology is the study of the structure of words and their parts (such as prefixes, roots, and suffixes) to understand what words mean. Etymology is the study of the origin of words and the way in which their meanings have evolved over time. When we combine instruction in them with vocabulary instruction, students' reading skills grow exponentially (Perfetti & Stafura, 2014; Kirby & Bowers, 2017).

Morphology

A morpheme is the smallest unit in a word that has meaning. Incorporating morphology into your teaching can pack a punch in building students' vocabulary. Here are two reasons why:

1. The majority of words students will encounter while reading contain morphemes, which they use as clues to the meaning of those words. As many as 60 percent of English

words "have relatively transparent morphological structure—that is, they can be broken down into [meaningful] parts" (Nagy et al., 1989).

2. Ninety percent of the words found in texts written in English come from about 2,500 word families (Hiebert et al., 2018). Once students learn the morphology of a key word, they can unpack the meaning of the rest of the words in that family. The maps of how words link to each other, broken out by the grade level at which each word first appears, are freely available as the Core Vocabulary Project.

Let's look at how you can integrate morphology into the teaching you're probably already doing. One great resource to help you, with a useful scope and sequence, is Heidi Anne Mesmer's *Big Words for Young Readers: Teaching Kids in Grades K to 5 to Decode—and Understand—Words With Multiple Syllables and Morphemes.*

Etymology

Paying attention to etymology can greatly boost your students' vocabulary because it can build their curiosity about words and their history. Again, any investigating you do will be helpful and you don't have to be a linguist. We weren't, nor were many of the teachers we've worked with. But we're nothing if not learners, a major factor in whatever successes we've had. Let's return to *The Cay* example from Chapter 2. Meredith admitted to the kids she wasn't sure what a cay was. She could have easily told the kids what it meant after looking it up. But admitting she didn't know something—specifically a word—modeled the humility and curiosity that's vital to a classroom that has an inquisitive approach to learning in general.

Morphemes live within every word. (Remember, they're the units that help convey meaning.) That fact is obviously important for helping to learn the meaning of unknown words (maybe you know what a part of the word means even if not the whole and this helps you figure the rest out). Equally important, in our estimation, is understanding that words *are* meaningful. They're literally *full of meaning*! Once students understand that, they'll be more likely to hunt for and expect meaning. This is a small but vital part of developing a successful reader's habit of mind, the topic of a later chapter. It's also a giant contributor to developing a deep sense of vocabulary, as we saw in Chapter 2.

Morphology in Action

Here are some basic morphemes worth teaching.

Common Morphemes			
Morpheme	**Meaning**	**Type**	**Examples**
un-	not/opposite of	prefix	unprepared, unable
-s, -es	more than one	suffix	students, books
spect	to look at	root	inspect, spectacle
re-	again or back	prefix	return, review
-ed	past tense (verbs)	suffix	watched, started
ject	to throw	root	reject, project
auto-	self	prefix	automatic, automobile
-er	one who…	suffix	baker, farmer, teacher
port	to carry	root	transport, portable

Modest, regular doses of morphology and etymology exploration will take your students' vocabulary a long way. You don't have to be or become an expert.

Mr. Morrisey, the teacher you met in Chapter 2, says this about teaching morphology: "I just love it because I can easily embed the teaching through content. For example, take the word *regenerated* as in the text, 'Wolves were reintroduced into Yellowstone. They helped curb the deer population and the deer moved to different locations so the vegetation regenerated in many parts of Yellowstone.' Students already knew that *gen* meant beginning and *re* meant again. Or teaching *peri* in fourth-grade math so students don't get *area* and *perimeter* mixed up, as *peri* means around. This kind of teaching can take less than a minute."

We hope you and your students become passionate about morphology, too, and if you do, that's great! We're arguing for regular exposure to words and building classroom cultures where curiosity is rewarded. Even if your students don't catch fire right away, *you* need to commit to staying curious about the words you and your students encounter when reading together. Don't fall into the trap of saying that English makes no sense or letting your students think that. We're arguing for establishing habits of inquiry and a culture of curiosity. Students should be able to make sense of what they read, down to the word level.

Encourage children to be curious about words and what they mean.

"Disaster" in the Classroom

One afternoon in Meredith's second-grade class, there was a fruit-juice spill during snacktime, and the mess upset the children at the table. Red spots wound up on some of their artwork. But nobody's clothes were stained and no real harm was done. Meredith said, "These things happen. It's not a disaster!" as she came over with a wet rag to wipe it up. All the kids had gotten quiet as they looked to see how bad the spill was, and Jacky wanted to know what *disaster* meant because she had heard the word on television about a recent earthquake near where her family had come from. Meredith promised to talk about the story of the word *disaster* tomorrow.

The next day, during morning meeting, she wrote *disaster* on the whiteboard and then wrote it like this: dis/aster. She said she'd read about the etymology of *disaster*, reminding the students that etymology meant the story of how the word came to be. The word had two parts: *dis* and *aster* and it came originally from the Greeks. She asked if they knew any words that had *dis-* at the front of them and they came up with a lot (*dissing, dislike, discover, disappear*). She asked if anyone knew what *dissing* was slang for. Jaime said his brother would always tell people who said "they were only dissing him" to stop disrespecting him, so it meant disrespecting.

Meredith asked Jacky if she had a guess what the *dis-* in *disaster* meant. She said she thought it meant not, like not trusting or respecting someone, and the class generally agreed. Meredith said *aster* was harder, but they might

know it in a different form, as *astro-*. They came up with *astronaut* and *asteroid* and the Houston Astros baseball team.

Meredith showed them a picture of an aster (a star-shaped flower), but they couldn't see the connection. So, she told them that *aster* was the Greek word for *star*, so a *disaster* meant a "bad star" or a star working against the world, and that was their word for when really bad things happened. A *disaster* was a terrible event, like the earthquake in Jacky's home country that had killed people and destroyed buildings, a natural disaster.

They finished by looking back at their other words: To *dislike* someone is the opposite of to like someone, *discover* means to not cover (hide). *Disappear* means to go away, whereas appear means to come into view. They saw that *dis-* always meant not or the opposite of the word it appeared in front of. That was supposed to be the end of *disaster*, but then someone asked about *distant*. Meredith wasn't sure that the meaningful parts worked the same way in that word and said so, but they needed to stop for now so it would need to wait.* She wrote it down and asked students to keep collecting those *dis-* words and they'd spend time looking them up at another time.

The payoff is always worth the time because it extends beyond the single word to the attitudes and beliefs we keep talking about. We hope you'll make the same word journeys with your students.

---

*It ends up *distant* and *distance* come from the Latin verb *distare*, itself made up of two morphemes: *di* meaning apart and *stare*, to stand. So *distant* means something that is standing apart or away. We circled back on that another day. So stay flexible and ready to learn when you're working with morphology. The English language has lots of interesting origin stories!

A Protocol for Teaching Morphology

Mr. Morrisey uses this protocol to directly teach morphemes that are important to his content goals and students' future learning.

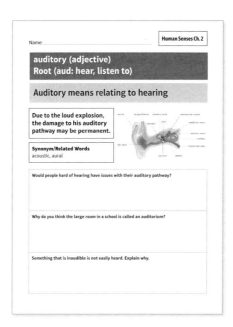
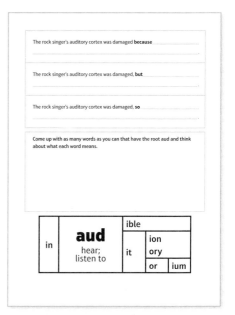

(Adapted from Bowers & Kirby, 2010)

Meredith developed another routine while working with Career and Technical Education students, many of whom had received poor reading instruction in their prior school experiences. But they had the enormous advantage of being immersed in the vocation they'd chosen, along with the specialized vocabulary of that vocation. (In fact, Meredith often needed her students to enlighten her on what, say, *micrometers* were.) All those words that convey important aspects of understanding that weren't part of their specialized vocabulary, however, often tripped her students up. So, she invented the "Mother of All Word Analysis."

KNOW BETTER, DO BETTER: COMPREHENSION

Meredith's "Mother of All Word Analysis" Routine

Similar to, but less formal than, the protocol on page 60, Meredith's routine gave students quick access to vital words they'd stumbled upon (and over) while reading. She developed it for secondary students, but it works well at any grade level.

A student reading aloud about properties of metals when heated couldn't decode the word *propensity*, and none of the other students knew what it meant. So, up it went on the whiteboard with syllable markers:

pro/pen/si/ty

She seized the opportunity to teach everyone that *-y* at the end of any word longer than one syllable is pronounced /e/. Once Meredith broke the word down, everyone could decode it, and she and the students read it aloud several times. Then she showed the morphemes and asked if anyone knew any of those parts:

pro- -pens- -ity

A few students suggested *pro-* meant forward or toward, like *prologue* or *propel*. Meredith told them that the ending *-ity* turns adjectives into nouns and gave some examples (*community*, *adversity*). They looked up the morphology of *propensity* because Meredith wasn't sure of its origins either, and found out it came from the Latin verb *pendere*, to hang or stretch. But a whole Latin word *propensus*, which means to incline to or hang toward, gave us the English word. Then they looked up the definition and found out it meant "a natural tendency or preference towards something." That fit with what they were reading about—the properties of metal that often cause it to warp when overheated. She then asked the students to pair up and use the word in a sentence about something they had a propensity for.

This all takes a few minutes, but it builds and reinforces in a pragmatic and simple way, all the ways of knowing a word. In this case, Meredith knew the decoding skills of her students were underdeveloped, and so she also supported some phonics reinforcement via the syllabication that made a formidable word more approachable. This is crucial for older readers with gaps in their foundational skills and reading confidence. It also reinforces the idea that reading is all about sensemaking, while insisting the students stop skipping over unfamiliar words they encounter. Whether they were second graders looking at *disaster* in Harlem or eleventh- and twelfth-grade tech students studying *propensity* in rural Vermont, students bought into these close examinations of a single word.

English spelling patterns are often driven by morphemes that are rooted in many languages. Written English is a river filled from the streams of many other peoples—at first caused by waves of invaders from elsewhere in Europe who colonized the British Isles. The Romans, the Norman French, and Greeks gave us a bunch of our Tier 3 words (and some of the most challenging spellings). That doesn't even begin to touch the words all our families and ancestors brought with them from their places and tongues of origin.

Etymology in Action

Here are some English words that came from peoples who have influenced the English language.

English Words Influenced by Waves of Invasions	Origin Language/Peoples
true, wife, house, this, laugh, tough	Anglo Saxon/Germanic Peoples
proud, beef, choice, very, table	French/Normans
agenda, common, popular, effect	Latin/Romans
democracy, dinosaur, music, biology	Greek/Age of Enlightenment Europe

Common American-English Words	Origin Language/Peoples
mosquito, patio, alligator, embargo	Spanish/Spanish settlers from Spain, Latin America, and other regions
caucus, chipmunk, pecan, toboggan	Various Indigenous Languages/North American nations
banjo, tote, jazz, cola	Primarily Bantu/Western Africans
chutzpah, bagel, klutz, shtick, maven	Yiddish/Eastern European Jews

All those words are spelled according to their original patterns. English is not consistently spelled according to its phonemes as some languages are. That's why you can have so many ways to make the long-*a* sound, or ridiculous looking ways to make an *f* sound (*-gh, ph-*). But that doesn't mean those patterns are arbitrary. Not at all! They are driven by the word's etymology, and learning about the origins of words can not only be fascinating, but helpful in conveying the vitality of English and the sense that underlies it.

🌐 That is why it is worthwhile to offer your students who speak languages other than English at home cognates from their home languages that map to English words they encounter while reading and discussing texts.

Two books deserve special mention. One is Wiley Blevins's *Teaching Phonics & Word Study in the Intermediate Grades, 3rd Edition* (2023). We're big fans of Wiley. He, like us, emphasizes the importance of providing students with enough repetition through practice so everybody can cement their learning. His book contains easy-to-implement morphology exercises that provide exposure to high-value Latin and Greek roots, along with high-frequency affixes. If you taught the morphology in his book and nothing else, you'd be helping your students enormously.

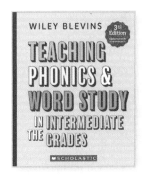

The other one is *Word Nerds: Teaching All Students to Learn and Love Vocabulary* by Brenda J. Overturf, Leslie H. Montgomery, and Margot Holmes Smith, a great addition to your resource collection. In addition to offering practical teaching advice, it is filled with joy. It does a fabulous job of modeling how fun it can be to become interested in words at a classroom or school level.

We invite you to explore other resources, on page 151. We've curated them carefully.

In Closing, Remember...

- The majority of words students encounter have recognizable morphemes—or meaningful units. Learning about morphemes grows vocabulary. It also increases and supports knowledge, as well as spelling and decoding skills.

- Learning about morphemes and etymology helps students see the logical structure underlying much of English. As such, it deepens their vocabulary.

- It also contributes to a culture in which words are valued, which has lots of payoffs.

While students are working to learn about the world and all the words that describe it, what can we do to help them comprehend what they read? What is going on in their minds as they read? What's the payoff for learning how that works? That's the topic of the next section, a deep dive into the nature of comprehension itself.

Ironically, comprehension, the whole point of reading, has been largely neglected in the science-of-reading conversation. We're aiming to change that with you.

PART II

WHAT YOU NEED TO KNOW TO FUEL THE READING BRAIN

CHAPTER 4

Comprehension: An Overview

"Reading comprehension" is a term we all use all the time in school. But what is it, really? Comprehension is something unto itself, but it is also everything that lies underneath it and contributes to developing complete understanding of text. We structured this book to reflect that truth. Everything that's come before this chapter—namely, the role of knowledge, vocabulary, morphology, and etymology—lies underneath successful reading comprehension.

But, traditionally, we don't teach reading with that understanding in mind. How is it that our instruction has strayed so far from the well-established science behind comprehension and what it means to comprehend? Even now, with the attention on phonics and the role of content knowledge, there is essentially nothing addressing how we get students to the end goal of all of reading instruction: an understanding of what they've read on their own and a clear sense of how they achieved that understanding.

This chapter explains what it means when the mind comprehends text. Let's begin with what comprehension is not.

Reading Comprehension Is Not Literature Discussion

Before the Common Core State Standards disrupted the norms back in 2010, nearly all reading in K–8 English Language Arts—that is, what we read to kids and what they read on their own—was fiction. Many of us came to equate reading with understanding themes, delving into characterization and plot, identifying settings, and appreciating literary devices such as metaphor, simile, and personification. And, by extension, so did our students. At Family Academy, we had students address questions around those concepts daily in literature groups. We weren't paying much attention at all to how students arrived at answers (and what was happening when they didn't). The discourse was about the elements of literature and, at its best, what we learned about ourselves and the world from what we read. That kind of discourse is good, but it isn't good enough. We weren't "peeking under the hood" to understand how our students' minds were processing texts. We weren't focusing on how they achieved an understanding of what they read from the reading itself. In short, we conflated reading and literature in our education ecosystem—and that informed how we approached reading.

> We weren't "peeking under the hood" to understand how our students' minds were processing texts. We weren't focusing on how they achieved an understanding of what they read from the reading itself.

Conflating reading and literature is still common practice in many schools today. Let's change that practice once and for all.

Again, comprehension is something unto itself, but it is also everything that lies underneath it. If students have weak word recognition, they can't be fluent, so sentences will not flow meaningfully for them, and they will struggle with comprehension. Some students may have proficient word recognition but can't read with fluency appropriate to the text. If they don't know the

meaning of many of the words they're encountering, or if they don't have the topic knowledge to fully comprehend parts of the text, or the ability to parse more complex ideas and connect them to earlier parts of the text, they will continue to struggle with comprehension.

But what if all those ingredients are in place for a reader? Is there something additional that needs to happen? Something we could name comprehension? There is, and to understand how to develop it in our students, we need to understand what it is.

Teachers often tell us that developing comprehension is the most frustrating part of ELA instruction. They know how high the stakes are but can't figure out what's misfiring for students who aren't making sense of what they read. Part II of this book is about figuring out what goes on in the brain when a reader is comprehending successfully so you know better what to do to help students get on track when their understanding falters.

Reading Comprehension Is an Extraordinary Process

Ask yourself to define *comprehension* without using a synonym for it, such as *understanding*, or the word itself. We've been trying this exercise for months, on and off, and haven't come up with the perfect definition yet.

Maybe that's because of how extraordinary the process of comprehension is. Think of all that goes into it. There are the foundational ingredients: phonemic awareness, decoding, automatic word recognition, and fluency. And then add these ingredients explained in Part I: syntax, word meanings, and the knowledge references we encounter in the pages of a text. All that awareness has to get integrated, sentence after sentence, into something meaningful. But that's not all. As you know from your own reading, readers continually upgrade their understanding as they move on down the page and through the whole text. And these things combine with one another and often are operating at the same time.

It's hard to capture all that in a single word!

Terms to Know

Here are some terms you'll need to know to navigate the rest of this book.

Comprehension is represented in the mind as a mental model at three levels:

1. **Surface Level:** the words in the text that readers must recognize and pronounce to read fluently. See Chapter 5, page 72, for details.

2. **Textbase:**
   - Macro level: the overall structure or organization of the text as a whole. See Chapter 5, page 73.
   - Micro level: the network of propositions or ideas in the text and how they connect to one another. See Chapter 5, page 75.

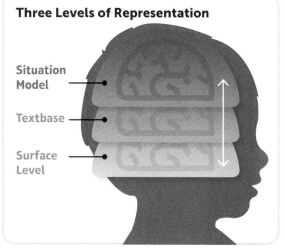

Three Levels of Representation

Situation Model

Textbase

Surface Level

3. **Situation Model:** the richest, most complete understanding of the text the reader can form. It's shaped by the reader's knowledge, experience, and even emotions. It goes beyond the textbase but doesn't invalidate it. It's more enduring than the recollection of the textbase alone. See Chapter 5, page 81.

Proposition: a single idea. A sentence can have multiple propositions, texts have many. Each idea in a sentence is a proposition.

Connectives: single words or short phrases that tie together two or more propositions. Connectives often carry clues as to what sort of connection the author is making.

Antecedents: the noun a pronoun is referring to.

Referents: any words or phrases that refer back to previous words or propositions. These are often pronouns, but not always.

In Closing, Remember...

- Comprehension is something unto itself, but it is also everything that lies underneath it and contributes to developing complete understanding of text.

- Foundational skills are essential to successful comprehension. Readers have to know or be able to figure out words in the text.

- Parsing meaning, sentence by sentence, and building meaning over the course of paragraphs and pages are key to comprehension.

- The terms in the "Terms to Know" section, on page 69, will be useful in the next chapter and thereafter.

There is a lot going on when it comes to reading comprehension! We're headed into the interior of the mind to learn about the mental modeling we know as comprehension. Once you have that understanding, you'll know better how to sort out students' misunderstandings and build sturdy readers.

Children engrossed in comprehending text.

Comprehension: A Deep Dive

R eading comprehension is not an observable skill. It's not even a cluster of observable skills, despite what assessments would have us believe.

Cognitive scientists refer to comprehension as "representation," meaning it is represented in our minds as a set of understandings. And it turns out that representation exists at three levels that continually and simultaneously build on, and interact with one another, as we read.

Three Levels of Text Representation in the Mind

Walter Kintsch's model (Kintsch & Kintsch, 2005; Kintsch, 2019) asserts that mental modeling happens at three levels. All the levels must be simultaneously active for comprehension to occur.

Let's look at each level closely before we look at how they integrate.

1. Surface Level

When we read at the surface level, we recognize the words in the text and read them fluently, even if we don't understand them. In other words, we apply foundational skills—decoding, word recognition, and fluency—including accounting for punctuation.

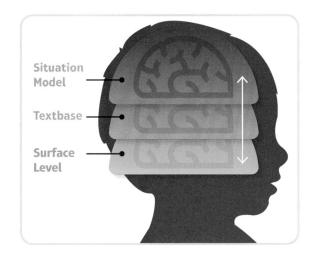

Consider the beginning of Lewis Carroll's poem "Jabberwocky" from *Through the Looking-Glass*:

Twas brillig and the slithy toves
Did gyre and gimble in the wabe;
All mimsy were the borogoves,
And the mome raths outgrabe.

Go ahead, read the words aloud quietly or as loud as you want, and notice how you naturally know how to pronounce each one. Read them again so they flow. You can pronounce the words and read the poem smoothly, but it has no meaning to you. You are reading at the surface level. In other words, what is in your mind are the visual representation of the "words" and the sound or auditory representation of the "words." You know the phonic patterns from knowing how to read English. You can string together the sounds each letter in *mimsy* makes, although you don't know what it means to be "mimsy." You can put all the words together and read them as the lines of poetry "Jabberwocky" is, even though, as Alice noted, "It seems very pretty, … but it's rather hard to understand." This is surface-level representation.

Watch David and Meredith explain the "Three Levels of Representation."

Readers can't have independent reading comprehension without being able to access text at the surface level. Though foundational skills aren't the focus of this book, their importance undergirds it. Readers need to have solid foundational skills to comprehend.

2. Textbase

The next level of mental representation is the textbase, which is made up of two distinct parts of the text, according to Kintsch (1998): the macrostructure and the microstructure.

The Macrostructure—Using the Text's Structure to Aid Understanding

The macrostructure is the overall structure of the text, or how it is organized. The macrostructure for narratives in Kintsch's terms consists of the setting, protagonists

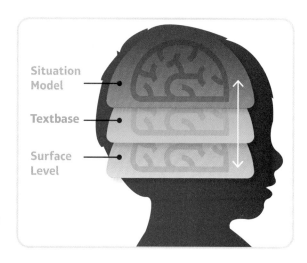

(actors or characters), problem or goal, intentionality (what the characters intend to do—intend because they don't always succeed), and the outcome (what happened whether intended or not). Non-narrative texts can have a variety of structures—problem/solution, cause/effect, goal/action/outcome, chronological, descriptive, generalization, and examples—and those structures can coexist in any combination across a single text. Understanding the macrostructure of a text helps a reader determine its most important ideas and the author's purpose. That explains why teaching students to attend to and recognize text structure, even in the primary grades, supports comprehension (Williams et al., 2016). But a little goes a long way. Here's a gift you rarely get in books about teaching and learning: a heap of time-and-energy saving!

We teachers spend a ton of time on narrative text structure because it's so concrete. We know exactly how to present it.

Too much time and too much focus. As the following story shows, students generally grasp it a lot better and more quickly than we give them credit for.

David was working in a second-grade classroom in Vermont. He wanted the kids to know more about stories—specifically, what they are, why humans like them so much, and why we have so many of them. The teacher spread out all the books the students had read or listened to so far that year, along with books they'd brought in from home. She then asked the students to work together to find a book that didn't have some kind of problem (it won't surprise you that the children remembered in uncanny detail the stories they'd been exposed to). It didn't take long before one little boy announced "Can't find any! If there's no problem, there's no story." This was followed by a discussion of other things all stories seem to share. And, very quickly, the students got all the narrative elements with barely any direct instruction from the adults.

Not only are story elements universal to the human experience, but many cognitive scientists now think we are hardwired to think in stories. Think about how readily we stitch a dream into a narrative (even if somewhat distorted) only to falter in trying to relay it to others. Similarly, kids get narrative structure quickly when we call on them to analyze it. They'll understand, just as quickly, why narrative text structure is easier to follow than non-narrative text structures.

Informational text structures, on the other hand, are not as intuitive and simple. But noticing and understanding them when encountered in context can assist comprehension. For example, if readers notice the information is structured as a problem-solution, they will first identify the problem and then have their antennae raised to look for the proposed solutions. If readers are aware they're reading a persuasive text, they'll be on the lookout for the

Young kids can grasp text structure readily.

KNOW BETTER, DO BETTER: COMPREHENSION

argument and compelling evidence. If readers know they're reading a description, they'll be aware that they should gather information that identifies what's being described.

But, there is wondrous variety in text structures, often even within one text. Texts often include multiple or blended structures. A text called "Overcoming Obstacles," for example, might include a series of obstacles someone overcame and also time-sequenced and descriptive elements. So recognizing text structure is a useful tool. In fact, reading researcher Joanna Williams shows that shifting focus in this deliberate manner (from an emphasis on narrative structures to the variety of structures) can enhance students' comprehension as early as second grade (Williams, 2005; Williams et al., 2016). But it can also be complicated, and that, too, is valuable for you and your students to be aware of. We explore more about how—and how much— to explore text structure with your students in Part III.

There is wondrous variety in text structures, often even within one text.

The Microstructure—Building Meaning, Proposition by Proposition

The microstructure is the text's line-by-line units of meaning and how they are stitched together. Each separate idea within every single sentence is called a *proposition* by cognitive scientists. This is where things get a little wonky, so hang on. Where the macrostructure is the organization of the text as a whole, the microstructure represents all the ideas within the text, how they connect to one another, and how those connections inform meaning. Bridging those line-by-line ideas, or propositions, to make meaning of the whole thing is the work of the reader.

PROPOSITIONS

A proposition and a sentence are different, contrary to what many of us were taught to believe—that a sentence contains one complete idea. You have to shake that idea to understand this section, and we appreciate the challenge of that! Here's an example to make the point that sentences can, and often do, contain more than one proposition:

> Sam wanted to go to the game but didn't want to disappoint her grandfather, who was expecting her.

Here we have three propositions:

1. Sam's desire (to go to the game)
2. Her reluctance to disappoint her grandfather
3. The idea that her grandfather was expecting her

Propositions, as you just saw, can be tightly connected to each other. The fact is, they can be connected in a variety of ways, which is not only what makes texts challenging, but also interesting.

Again, a proposition is one single idea in a sentence and within the text. Even a picture book has dozens and dozens of propositions within it. Sentences containing multiple propositions present obstacles to comprehension, and we talk about this and what to do to support student understanding much more in the next section.

CONNECTIVES

Connections between propositions can be explicit, with the author clearly signaling to the reader how one proposition connects to another, or more implicit, leaving it to the reader to figure out (infer) the connections.

When a reader successfully connects propositions in a text, psychologists call that a "bridging inference." Frequently, the author helps readers out by using words and phrases that signal explicit connections. The formal name for these, not surprisingly, is *connectives* (e.g., *in addition, even though, because, as we saw earlier*). Connectives are

---

Types of Connectives

- **Causal:** *because, consequently, as a result, thus…*
- **Temporal:** *later, afterwards, earlier, during…*
- **Sequential:** *first, second, next, last, from here on…*
- **Additive:** *additionally, furthermore, moreover, both, what's more…*

- **Adversative:** *but, however, yet, although, nevertheless.* Adversatives can be especially important, as they completely change the direction of the text by connecting two ideas that don't go together in some way, as in "The baseball game was fun but way too long."

---

helpful to the reader because they signal relationships between the propositions or ideas. That is, they're helpful if our students know what a given connective is signaling and can be on the lookout for them. Cultivating this level of alertness is especially helpful for multilingual learners and we explore several ways to do this in the next section.

In sum, connectives help readers make bridging inferences across the text's network of propositions. The more connectives there are, and the closer the words, phrases, and clauses being connected are, the more they support comprehension of the textbase—provided readers understand what the connectives mean and the work they're doing.

What factors make it more or less difficult to make inferences? What can this process of sorting it out look like? We use text excerpts in the charts on the next few pages to show you, and hopefully begin to answer questions you may have.

Inferencing: What Is It?

When students make connections between and among propositions as they read, they are making inferences. That's true whether they make them with the support of connective words or not. Even if connectives are present, readers still have to cue themselves to do the work of making the connection between the ideas. The presence of connectives just makes the job easier. Again, that's if the reader notices them.

Making inferences while reading is a skill. Numerous studies (Soto et al., 2019; Kendeou et al., 2016; Kintsch, 2019; Cain et al., 2001) have shown that students who make inferences are more proficient readers. What they're doing is connecting the propositions in the text. They're doing it efficiently and accurately. To spread this ability to everyone means creating lots of opportunities to read texts that require frequent inferencing. Having students explain their thinking will strengthen their ability to make inferences. This self-explanation is one of the most powerful instructional moves we'll be exploring in depth in the next section.

Bridging to Propositions Within the Text

Best-selling Books Began With a Bedtime Story	Source Text—Context	Cohesion Feature(s) That Are Helping or Hurting
Haley Riordan was not interested in many of the subjects they taught him in school. But he loved Greek mythology and one night he asked his dad to tell him bedtime stories about the Greek gods and heroes. "I had taught Greek myths for many years at the middle school level so I was glad to comply," says Riordan. "When I ran out of myths, [Haley] was disappointed and asked me if I could make up something new with the same characters." According to Riordan, his journey into the world of kids' books began with that request. Using Greek mythology as a springboard, Riordan came up with a character named Percy Jackson, the half-human, half-god son of Poseidon, Greek god of the sea. "It took about three nights to tell the whole story and when I was done, Haley told me I should write it out as a book." As a salute to Haley, who had been diagnosed with ADHD and dyslexia, Riordan chose to give Percy those challenges, too … "It's not a bad thing to be different. Sometimes it's the mark of being very, very talented."	Rick Riordan is a best-selling author of several series, including the Percy Jackson and the Olympians series. Here, he is telling the origin story of Percy Jackson. He had been a middle school English teacher for many years when he started telling his son, Haley, the bedtime story that became the first Percy Jackson book, *The Lightning Thief*. This excerpt is from a 2016 profile of Riordan.	Both Rick Riordan and his son Haley are mentioned nine times with the same set of pronouns (he/him/his). This could confuse even a mature reader. At the same time, this is both the story of how the Percy Jackson books came to be and an interview with their author. The frequent use of first person when the article quotes directly from Rick Riordan adds another layer of pronoun-antecedent complexity to tracking the propositions within this passage. The word *request* in the third paragraph refers to Haley asking his dad for stories about the Greek gods. This is an important bridge between these two propositions for readers since it is the origin story for this well-beloved series of books. A subtle connection is made between Haley's not liking much in school and the information in the last paragraph that he has been diagnosed with ADHD and dyslexia. If readers don't know what they are, they wouldn't know how uncomfortable having these challenges can make school for some people.

When students fail to make a bridging inference, you'll need to explore by asking why they think they didn't understand. Only by posing questions that require students to make these connections and explain their answers will we know for sure *why* they went astray. We'll discuss how to do that in the next part of the book.

Text Excerpt	Source Text—Context	Cohesion Feature(s) That Are Helping or Hurting
We have gathered here to affirm a faith, a faith in a common purpose, a common conviction, a common devotion. Some of us have chosen America as the land of our adoption; the rest have come from those who did the same. For this reason, we have some right to consider ourselves a picked group, a group of those who had the courage to break from the past and brave the dangers and the loneliness of a strange land.	This excerpt is from the opening of Judge Learned Hand's 1944 address at a swearing-in ceremony for new citizens.	In the second sentence, *us* refers to those who have chosen to immigrate to America, as noted in the first sentence, *the rest* refers to the children of those who came to America voluntarily. In the next sentence, *we* represents both groups combined. Unless this chain of connections is followed, the paragraph can't really be understood. The pronouns could make this difficult but so could the density of propositions. So, too, could the lengthy sentences. The reader (listener) can't know who the judge is addressing without making those connections.

Developing these examples was a challenge to us as adult readers, due to a couple of factors crucial to students attaining successful reading comprehension.

1. Often, as mature readers, *we* see the connections between propositions from one part of a text to another so automatically, we don't even notice them, let alone that they can confound our students. That's why overlooking connections is dangerous when we're considering texts for our students to read. That seamless connecting may not be occurring for many of our students. As Cain and Oakhill's (1999, 2006) work has shown, this can happen to students even when they have the knowledge the text requires, and even when they can recall aspects of the text accurately.

2. Even if a student fails to make a connection or two, it doesn't necessarily mean he or she loses the thread of the text. Maybe he or she falters and recovers or loses the thread further along in his or her reading from an accumulation of confusions. But that's hard to see until the student is well into the text, and more likely to happen if he or she is confused early on, so we need to be especially watchful for confusions that develop early. Even if failing to make connections doesn't fatally

affect comprehension, students could lose opportunities to grow their knowledge of words and the world.

Text Cohesion and Propositions—How Ideas in the Text Connect

Cohesion, as used by cognitive psychologists, is the collection of a text's elements that helps readers comprehend. To form a successful sense of the textbase, a reader needs to connect the text's propositions, or idea units. How difficult that is for the reader depends largely on the text's cohesion. In general, the more cohesion a text has, the easier it is to read. There are two broad categories of cohesion: local and global.

LOCAL COHESION

Local cohesion is the repetition of text elements (e.g., words, phrases, and clauses) from sentence to sentence (Graesser et al., 2003). The closer those elements are, the easier the text is to read. Let's see how that plays out in Chapter Two of Cynthia Rylant's *Missing May*.

> May was *gardening* when she died. That's the word she always used: *gardening*. Everyone else in Fayette County would say they were going out to work in the garden, and that's the picture you'd get in your mind—people out there laboring and sweating and grunting in the dirt. But Aunt May *gardened*, and when she said it your mind would see some lovely person in a yellow-flowered hat snipping soft pink roses, little robins landing on her shoulder.
>
> Of course May never owned a flowered hat in her life, and her garden was as practical as anyone else's. In place of roses it was full of thick pole beans and hard green cabbages and strong carrots. It was a reliable garden, and friendly, and both Ob and me finally thought it right that May should have flown up out of her body right there in that friendly garden, among all those cheerful vegetables, before she waved goodbye to us and went on to be that bright white Spirit Ob had known all along she was.
>
> Only this part of her death seemed right. The garden. (pp. 10–11)

This passage is highly coherent. Here's why: Rylant is returning to the topic of May's sudden death, a hard topic for many readers. Here, she elaborates on that death, explaining where May died and why that is a comfort. May died in her beloved garden, a fact readers are reminded of by the word appearing eight times in various forms. Rylant uses May's name frequently, too. She places pronouns close to May's name to make them easy to track. All that helps readers connect propositions involving May. We were introduced to Summer, the young first-person narrator, in Chapter One. Here, Summer is talking about how Ob and she felt about May dying in the garden, so Rylant renames them us or "Ob and me" a couple of times. Those are more pronouns readers have to track. Though Rylant makes them as straightforward as she can, pronouns always have the potential to be comprehension stumbling blocks.

As we wrote this book, particularly this complicated chapter, we, too, tried to provide lots of local cohesion because we know many of our ideas may be new to readers. That hopefully makes the propositions more accessible.

GLOBAL COHESION

Global cohesion refers to the links the writer uses between larger sections of text, that are also likely to be further apart from one another (Givón, 1995; Ericsson & Kintsch, 1995). It covers a variety of allusions authors use that might be scattered across chapters more widely than local cohesion features would be. They also might be whole phrases that remind you of what came before (or what's coming up). Some examples are phrases like "in addition to," "as we saw earlier," and "another cause." They can also be the same words that signal connection for local cohesion (*because, however, later*).

The difference between global and local cohesion has to do largely with how far apart the references are from each other. To fully comprehend what they're reading, students must be able to connect ideas the author intends for them to understand, regardless of their proximity to one another.

3. Situation Model

Remember, Kintsch's model of comprehension operates simultaneously at three levels.

The situation model is the richest, most complete understanding of the text the reader can form. It's shaped by the reader's knowledge, experience, and even emotions. It goes beyond the textbase but doesn't invalidate it. It's more enduring than the recollection of the textbase alone.

But this is not a linear process. Just as word recognition and fluency work in parallel with comprehension, as a reader comprehends the textbase he or she is simultaneously growing and adjusting their situation model.

The situation model transfers what has been read from short-term to long-term memory, making it what is primarily retained by the reader. It is that deeper, fuller understanding of what has been read that is integrated into a reader's ever-evolving knowledge base. So, the situation model is how the text is ultimately represented in the mind, in its fullest version. Unlike the surface level or textbase, readers will use the situation model when recalling the text in the future. It's important to understand that the situation model develops and adjusts simultaneously with the other levels as the reader processes the text.

Unlike the surface level or textbase, readers will use the situation model when recalling the text in the future.

Essentially, the difference between the situation model and the textbase is the addition of the reader's existing relevant knowledge, which both enriches and clarifies understanding. That knowledge can come from what the reader already has, or knowledge newly gained earlier from the text. Knowledge doesn't replace the textbase, but rather adds nuance, richness, and context. In a sense, it elaborates on the textbase. Let's look at some examples.

Consider two upper-elementary students, both solid readers, reading a passage on hibernation. Each student can access the surface level and the textbase. Each is noticing and connecting the relevant propositions (e.g., how an animal's metabolism slows down during hibernation; what adaptive advantages hibernation offers; dangers from predators while an animal is hibernating). Both students can incorporate the structure of the text, its purpose, examples, and central ideas, as well as many of its details.

But the student who had read several informational texts about bears, or a story about children accidentally finding a turtle hibernating in the mud, or was familiar with animals that hibernate from reading books or watching shows on nature would know more. This student would develop a richer and more nuanced situation model from the same text. The other student didn't know much about hibernation. In fact, everything he knew he learned from the current text. He doesn't have as much topic knowledge to bring to the text, but he's a careful reader who gleans everything he can from it.

The Power of Personal Experiences

While working with a rural middle school, David learned how a student's experience dramatically impacted his situation model. The class was reading an article about a U.S. military family who lost their mother while she was stationed in Iraq. The article was particularly relevant to one student whose mother was deployed in Iraq. In nearly all the discussions, the student was quiet, dutifully doing the assignments even though the teacher, who was aware of the situation, had offered to let him opt out. Toward the end of the final lesson, he spoke at length, eloquently comparing his experiences with the family in the article. Needless to say, every student was captivated.

What struck David and the teacher was how this student's willingness to participate led to a richer situation model for all his classmates. His layered knowledge had expanded and enriched everyone's understanding. All students benefited from building their own situation model while hearing about their classmate's deeper, richer situation model. This was socially constructed comprehension. It was powerful to witness and resulted in everyone developing an enriched situation model.

Experiences can inform a situation model, including, as this story makes clear, emotional, personal experiences.

Constructing a Situation Model by Bridging Inferences to Knowledge

Connectives support the formation of robust situation models, even if the reader might be lacking some knowledge. Let's look again at *Missing May* to see how that works. This chart shows a possible situation model for the passage shown on page 80.

Passage from *Missing May*	Possible Situation Model
May was *gardening* when she died. That's the word she always used: *gardening*. Everyone else in Fayette County would say they were going out to work in the garden, and that's the picture you'd get in your mind—people out there laboring and sweating and grunting in the dirt. But Aunt May *gardened*, and when she said it your mind would see some lovely person in a yellow-flowered hat snipping soft pink roses, little robins landing on her shoulder.	May died in her vegetable garden. She loved gardening, so that was a little bit of comfort for her small family: Ob, her husband, and the narrator [Summer], her great niece, who missed her so badly.
Of course, May never owned a flowered hat in her life, and her garden was as practical as anyone else's. In place of roses, it was full of thick pole beans and hard green cabbages and strong carrots. It was a reliable garden, and friendly, and both Ob and me finally thought it right that May should have flown up out of her body right there in that friendly garden, among all those cheerful vegetables, before she waved goodbye to us and went on to be that bright white Spirit Ob had known all along she was.	
Only this part of her death seemed right. The garden. (pp. 10–11)	

Readers who read Chapter One know by the time they reach this passage in Chapter Two that May is dead and her small family is missing her terribly. They also know that May and Ob made a loving home for their orphaned great niece, Summer, for the past six years, even though they have little money. Nonetheless, this short passage portrays May as a rich character for readers who can follow how seriously and lovingly she approached her vegetable gardening. Readers who know something about gardening and growing food probably understand the difference between a flower garden and a vegetable garden. They know flower gardens exist to provide pleasure and beauty, whereas vegetable gardens provide food. These gardens can help nourish a family and are often grown by country people who have real need for what the garden brings to the family table. Those readers are in a better position to understand the difference between "working in the garden" and "gardening." They'll likely form a coherent textbase easily as they read. In other words, they'll connect all of the text's propositions, or idea units, as they encounter them.

Similarly, readers who have heard of or have some sense of an afterlife would be able to understand "...it was right that May should have flown up out of her body right there [in the friendly garden]" as a reference to eternal life for the

human spirit after a person dies. Those readers might not be as bewildered at the image of May waving goodbye to them as a reader who doesn't have any sense of afterlife's meaning through reading or learning they have done in other settings.

Students need to read about familiar and unfamiliar topics.

Readers who don't know about gardening, and who do not understand those expressions, would have to work a lot harder to make bridging inferences to form a coherent textbase. For example, suppose students were familiar with flower and vegetable gardens, but had never read about or experienced how hard it can be to keep them healthy and growing. They'd be puzzled by the contrast Summer draws between someone who gardens and someone "out there laboring and sweating and grunting in the dirt." They could make a bridging inference that would help them understand the difference between people who can afford to garden as a hobby vs. people who must work to grow food. At the same time, they would gain insight into the special person May was. She made her necessary work a labor of love and created a "friendly," "reliable" vegetable garden. Furthermore, readers with no knowledge of the afterlife could read and understand Summer and Ob's thinking about part of May as living on above them as a "bright white Spirit."

Reading remains the most efficient way to acquire and grow knowledge. Read a lot, learn a lot!

Proficient readers can make bridging inferences to develop a textbase and situation model, even if they lack some of the relevant knowledge. Rylant leaves lots of breadcrumb clues for readers in this passage. Let's look at how an alert reader can use such clues to bridge propositions to other propositions to grow new knowledge.

By doing the work of comprehending, students will learn the meaning of unfamiliar concepts. When Rylant makes the distinction between working in a garden and gardening in the first paragraph, she shifts to the *you* pronoun. She says about working in the garden: "...that's the picture you'd get in your mind—people out there laboring and sweating and grunting in the dirt." She uses a form of *you* when she shifts to gardening: "...when she said it your mind would see some lovely person in a yellow-flowered hat snipping soft pink roses, little robins landing on her shoulder." Why? She's providing us with the visual she wants us to see in our mind and helps us get it by using *you* and *your*. This is unusually directive writing that supports the reader who may not, in fact, have a clear sense of various kinds of gardening. And it is lovely, really, because we also learn something about May. She does the hard and vital work of vegetable gardening but finds the pleasure and joy of someone gardening for fun.

This is one example of how much a reader learns from reading and why doing it remains the most efficient way to acquire and grow knowledge. Read a lot, learn a lot!

But there's a caveat here that links back to the importance of knowledge. Bridges have two bases at a minimum, not one. If readers don't have enough knowledge to form at least one of the bases, their comprehension can break down completely. You can see how easily this could happen to a student just learning English who's working through the language demands of a text, or a child who has never before read or seen anything about gardening of any sort, nor had any direct experience with spiritual beliefs about death.

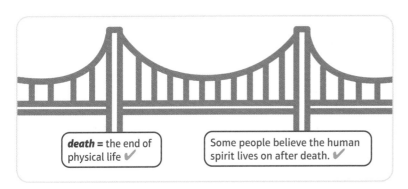

The student who knows about gardening and is familiar with ideas of life after death will automatically and effortlessly make a bridging inference. The majority of inferences proficient readers make happen so quickly that they're hard to trace. The student who knows what death is but doesn't know what on earth a person "flying up out of their body" means will have to infer its meaning from the two references. The good news is if our young readers can do that, they will learn so much by working through all these propositions.

Be aware that the time and effort required by students can slow the reading process. If inferring becomes too challenging and time-consuming, students may have a hard time remembering information that came before the point at which they're trying to make the inference. Our short-term (working) memories can only do so much. That is one reason knowledge is so important to comprehension. Having no knowledge is akin to having a half-built bridge. And if students aren't acquiring and growing it, there's no payoff to reading because it takes too much effort. Students experiencing that overload need a helping hand from us, their teachers. That's one of the things we value about close reading. Students stay close to the text and work with it in various ways, while they're carefully coached. They focus on the text and each other's ideas about it; the teacher stays close to their thought processes so he or she knows when to provide an assist.

But not too fast with that support! Don't preempt student effort. It's important to remember everyone encounters ideas they don't fully understand when they read. That's true if what they read is sufficiently rich. So, it is essential for students to know what to do and to have the self-discipline and confidence to dig in and try, before we step in. More on this, and on how close reading can achieve these outcomes, in Chapter 7.

How does all this relate to students developing situation models? We want to show you the variations that can arise for different students.

The situation model we laid out for the *Missing May* passage is pretty bare bones. A student with no gardening knowledge and minimal exposure to beliefs about life after death might have this kind of bare-bones situation model upon reading this section of *Missing May*, but a student who has gardening experience or who's read about growing vegetables, and is aware of spiritual beliefs about the afterlife, might develop a situation model with more skin on its bones. They might visualize a "friendly" vegetable garden they know, or they may have deep emotional responses to May's death in her garden, or make connections to other stories or life experiences. Doing those things would add nuance and richness to their developing model, as they work to make sense of the textbase.

The texts we give students to read should provide both types of opportunities: ones that connect to what they know so they can glide along relatively easily, and ones that present unfamiliar topics and ideas that require them to work harder to comprehend. If we do this regularly, our instruction can drive educational equity every single day because we understand what it takes for our students to build solid mental models. Remember those mirrors, windows, and sliding glass doors (Bishop, 1990)? Having a variety of texts that call on expansive and diverse knowledge is essential to all students if they are to flourish as learners and readers.

To sum up, the amount of knowledge a reader possesses plays a significant, threefold role in comprehension:

1. If students possess rich knowledge about what they're reading, they may effortlessly make bridges to relevant knowledge, and develop the more robust situation model, but may learn less *new* knowledge from the reading.

2. If students possess some knowledge of the topic, bridging inferences will be more effortful and time-consuming. Students may emerge with a less robust situation model, but may gain the most facility in making inferences from their hard work. They may also grow more knowledge from their efforts. They, along with everyone involved, will benefit greatly from engaging in rich discussions that address this process.

3. If students possess too little knowledge, they may not be able to use the text to grow knowledge while they read and will be more likely to lose the thread of the text, unless they get some support from discussion or other assists to fill those gaps.

Students need to be exposed to a wide variety of texts, which includes texts read independently, texts read with support, and from being read to (especially early in life and in early school years). Imagine being read *Missing May* in fourth grade and then encountering it again in middle school, so all the details of a close-knit family that has lost its center become part of students' knowledge. As we've seen, when students are exposed to texts that draw upon something they've read or know about from their own experiences, they are more likely to make the inferences they need to tie together the textbase and develop a richer, more nuanced situation model. Those texts are usually easier for those students to read. When we give students texts that are less reflective of their lived experiences or knowledge, they exercise the cognitive muscles they need to make those more difficult bridging inferences.

This is an area where equity and the science of reading come together. If students have a diet of texts largely reflecting their lived experiences, they are likely to use their inferencing muscles less. If students have a diet of texts outside of their lived experiences, they need to use—and further develop—their inferencing muscles. But that can only happen if they have at *least some of the knowledge needed to make the inferences*. Students who don't have the knowledge needed can't make the necessary inference. They lose the thread of the text, can't grow new knowledge, and don't exercise their inferencing muscles. That reading experience hasn't profited them at all.

This is why a steady diet of texts outside the lived experience of students has done so much damage for generations of readers. Too many texts too far outside students' lived experiences will not allow for knowledge to be gained, or for inferencing to be successful unless some significant scaffolding is put in place to support understanding. But students who have been overly represented in the texts they're exposed to are net losers, too. Texts that don't require any work to make inferences because the subject matter is overly familiar won't grow inferencing muscles either.

The next section explains the importance of providing ample opportunities for all students to develop the habits and tendencies to do that hard work for themselves.

Developing a Strong Standard of Coherence

A body of research called "Standard of Coherence" helps to explain why readers may possess knowledge but not use it while reading.

Students with a high Standard of Coherence are more likely to notice if their understanding of what they're reading is breaking down. They'll stop to repair whatever is interfering. Knowing that, and that this is a habit that can be reinforced, we can cultivate a high Standard of Coherence. Toward that end, students can be taught to pay attention to their understanding and to do something about it if they aren't (essentially to employ the vital strategy of comprehension monitoring) as a regular part of reading. This will help develop the habits that will lead to a strong Standard of Coherence, especially when they are given lots of chances to process text in the company of peers and when you, their teacher, insist on and expect "stick-with-it-ness" from them.

Standard of Coherence: What Is It?

Standard of Coherence is a reader's expectation that he or she will understand what he or she reads and is willing to work for that understanding (Oudega & van den Broek, 2018). Graesser et al. (1994) note that when their Standard of Coherence is high, readers are more likely to work in search of the coherence they expect to find. Conversely, Ferreira et al. (2002) note that when their Standard of Coherence is low, readers are more likely to be satisfied with a "good enough" sense of what they read.

In Closing, Remember...

- Reading comprehension doesn't develop by simply asking students to read literature.
- Foundational skills, vocabulary, knowledge, and syntax underlie successful comprehension but most instruction doesn't reflect the ways these features interact.
- Professional learning typically does not address how to teach reading in a way that allows teachers to see why students are not comprehending.
- Comprehension is represented in the mind at three levels: surface level, textbase level, and situation model.
    - The **surface level** is decoding, word recognition, and fluency.
    - The **textbase** has two parts: the macrostructure and the microstructure. The macrostructure is the overall text structure.

The microstructure is the network of propositions or ideas in the text and how they are connected.

- The **situation model** is the more holistic comprehension of the text, shaped by the reader's knowledge, experience, and emotions in combination with his or her reading of the textbase.

- Successful comprehension requires the reader to connect propositions to one another and to relevant background knowledge.

- Awareness of connective words and phrases and knowing what they mean are particularly helpful to multilingual learners.

- A reader's Standard of Coherence is the extent to which he or she expects to comprehend—and work at—all that a text has to offer. Proficient readers have a higher Standard of Coherence.

Comprehension is holistic and interactive. There are a lot of processes in play simultaneously when we read. Reading comprehension comes about when readers absorb a text's individual propositions and grasp the relationships between and among them. This forms their understanding of the textbase. At the same time, readers use relevant knowledge to clarify and enrich those understandings and form their situation model. All that provides the comprehensive understanding we know as reading comprehension. It's not about checking off skills or scouring a text for details to answer questions.

Unfortunately, current instruction and assessment too often veer away from this dynamic integrated process in favor of a narrow focus on skills and standards. Shifting instruction away from that focus requires putting text at the center of classroom discourse and working (sometimes together, sometimes on one's own) to develop a full understanding of the text. In Part III, we show you examples and look closely at instruction that develops the abilities and habits of mind to do just that.

PART III

WHAT YOU CAN DO TO FUEL THE READING BRAIN

CHAPTER 6

The Power of Questions and Centering the Text

So many elements are embedded in and contribute to successful comprehension. Here are the elements we've explored thus far: the role of knowledge, vocabulary, and morphology and etymology. And we looked at how solid instruction in those elements helps us improve children's ability to comprehend texts.

We looked at how comprehension is represented in our minds at the surface level, in the textbase, and in the situation model. Though this book doesn't directly address foundational skills, it stresses their importance and how essential they are to comprehension.

In this chapter, we focus on the power of asking text-based questions and why it's crucial to always expect students to explain how they arrived at their answers as they read and work with complex grade-level text. We then talk about why most current approaches to improving reading comprehension don't work.

Questions as the Comprehension Centerpiece

Text-based question asking is key to developing students' curiosity and helping them unpack texts—particularly the tricky parts or the parts that illuminate meaning most. That's because, in many ways, artful questioning is the key to the whole comprehension vault. It's certainly our main tool, as educators, to see what our students have in fact grasped and where their understanding needs more support.

There's a deep research base for questioning the text as an avenue to comprehension (Beck et al., 1996), whether teachers pose questions to students or students pose questions about the text directly. The more opportunities students have to practice questioning the text themselves and then doing what's known as self-explanation—essentially working through the text evidence that helps them come to an answer (Bisra et al., 2018; Pressley et al., 1992)—the better their own habits of monitoring for understanding will be. That ability is pivotal. But how they *learn* to do that can and should be a highly social process.

It's crucial to always expect students to explain how they arrived at their answers as they read and work with complex grade-level text.

Jacky, one of our most memorable students, struggled mightily to be the reader she wanted to be. She, her mom, her older sister, and younger brother were all refugees from Central America. Jacky started in our first class in kindergarten and had learned spoken English largely from interactions with the other kids. Her life had been unsettled for a long time and her mom and older sister hadn't been in a position to cultivate literacy at home in any language. Of anyone we ever worked with, Jacky may have been the hungriest to excel at reading for understanding. She listened carefully to her classmates' explanations of how they'd arrived at their answers, and always followed along as they reread the textual evidence and explained their thinking. Doing that improved Jacky's fluency and built her understanding of how to read that way. She gradually became aware of what caused her comprehension to break down when it did—generally when she encountered English vocabulary she didn't know—and could name the source of confusion and ask for clarification. In short, Jacky took in all the information exchanged orally each day and gradually became the reader she aspired to be.

Proving Your Answer

How did we know which students had which problems? And what did we do about it?

For starters, we started asking students to explain why they'd answered a given question as they did. We called that "Proving Your Answer."

Proving Your Answer became our students' superpower. We asked (actually, *required*) them to explain their answers. And students in every classroom, from Grade 2 to Grade 8, knew they might be called on to do so. This enabled teachers to see what was going on with students and what kinds of problems, if any, they were having. If the student explained his or her answer accurately and thoroughly, modeling his or her thinking for the rest of the class or group, we knew that student was on track. (Modeling was what helped Jacky so much.) If a student explaining ran into a dead end, the teacher could move in to address what had gone wrong. By addressing that student's error pattern, we educated students who were listening as well.

Students must have plenty of opportunity to address questions individually, orally and in writing. We eventually want them able to self-explain

independently. Individual efforts can, of course, be followed by turn and talks, pair/shares, or similar activities to capture the benefits and satisfaction of social learning. We can't overestimate the value of students learning to "self-explain" to becoming strong, self-regulated readers who read for understanding. A *lot* of research backs this recommendation (Chi et al., 1989; Chi et al., 1994; Cho & Jonassen, 2012; McNamara, 2017). Make sure you give your students regular chances to investigate their responses to questions so they can explain them to themselves, their classmates, and you.

We've seen in many classrooms the collective insights a rich, text-based discussion can promote. Such classrooms are lively, intellectually stimulating places. Good questions can direct students' time and attention to what is most critical for understanding. An environment that welcomes student-centered discussions will ensure that everyone has access to the learning and insights gleaned by any one student. As we think through all the elements that go into successful comprehension, we can't lose sight of how crucial it is to provide students with the time and supportive space to express their wonderings and questions aloud to each other, *and* in written form for themselves. We must insist that students listen to one another and build on each other's insights and explanations. That is a classroom that truly floats everyone's boat and leads to improved outcomes for each student.

Questions are powerful diagnostic tools. They can help you determine whether students:

- understand specific words in the text that transmit important information.
- are connecting propositions to their relevant knowledge.
- are connecting propositions across the text.
- need help with knowledge demands in the text.
- are struggling to understand the author's purpose or text's theme.
- understand the overall structure of the text and are using that understanding to aid comprehension.
- are following the text's transitions.
- are not comprehending the text because of language they haven't yet mastered.

Each Text Is a Frozen Kaleidoscope of Unique Features

This list of features gives you a picture of what could be inside any rich, complex text, regardless of genre or type:

- Lack of words, sentences, or paragraphs that review or summarize key points for the student
- Longer paragraphs
- A text structure that is less narrative and/or mixes structures
- Subtle and/or frequent transitions
- Concepts and ideas that are implied but not stated
- Multiple and/or subtle purposes or themes
- Density of information
- Unfamiliar settings, topics, or events
- Lack of repetition, few connectives or overlap between propositions
- Complex sentences
- Less common or even obscure vocabulary

The presence and interactions of those features determine a text's complexity and how difficult the text might be for a reader. For example:

- A text may contain complex syntax, but the difficulty may be reduced because the author employs simple vocabulary.
- Conversely, a text may contain sophisticated vocabulary, but in the context of simpler sentences or less demand for preexisting knowledge.
- Another text may be packed with information, but the author describes that information using simple vocabulary and supplies text features like bullets or numbering that help the reader parse the information.
- Still another may have multiple purposes, but the author includes clear connectors that help the reader tie those purposes together.

Each text is essentially a frozen kaleidoscope, presenting its own combination of features and its own unique degree of challenge. The possibilities are nearly endless. It is those interactions that make texts more or less complex.

11! (Eleven Factorial)

We shift to a fun math concept for just a moment to explain why questioning text is an effective way to help students access it.

Focusing on the features of a text tells us what, specifically, is contributing to its complexity. Assuming that any of these features could be present in *any* text in *any* combination, that's a lot of possibilities!

Mathematicians have named the formula to calculate the total number of possible combinations "factorials." The formula tells us that the number of different ways a text can be complex is 11 x 10 x 9 x 8 x 7 x 6 x 5 x 4 x 3 x 2 x 1. That is 11 factorial (expressed *most appropriately* as 11!) and is equal to 39,916,800.

That is why we focus on the text in planning, not this list of features or *any* other standalone list of strategies or standards to be "covered." Let the text reveal the features it contains in unique combinations that make it rich and worthwhile.

It's also why, if you only have time to do one thing to prepare for teaching comprehension, hands down, read the text you're going to be working with. Carefully. Every text—every passage—provides its own unique set of challenges. Ask your questions around those challenges.

When it comes to instruction, we must teach ourselves to notice and focus on the most challenging features of each text that we're considering for students. Then we must teach students to do the same *and* how to handle those features so they can understand what they're reading—text by text. Each text offers new riches and new ways for readers to glean its meaning.

Watch David and Meredith discuss the metaphor of the Frozen Kaleidoscope.

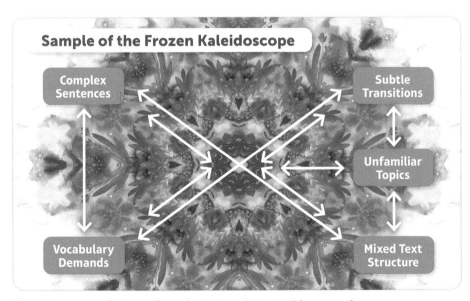

Sample of the Frozen Kaleidoscope

- Complex Sentences
- Subtle Transitions
- Unfamiliar Topics
- Vocabulary Demands
- Mixed Text Structure

This is just one way features of complex text can interact with one another.

Text Features as the Basis of Instruction

If our goal is for students to comprehend the text, as it should be, we need to always keep an eye out for where and why they go astray. It's a mistake to focus on any one text feature to the exclusion of others because the difficulty of that feature is determined by the way it interacts with every other feature. If a student gets a sequence question wrong, it probably isn't because he or she doesn't understand what sequence is. It's probably because some other text feature(s) tripped him or her up. If we focus too much on sequence, we might attribute the student's failure to misunderstanding sequence because we're not open to, and curious about, what else may be causing the problem.

To avoid those struggles, we must be aware of what's going on in the text and what might be tripping points for our students. And a good place to start is by asking students to explain what gave them trouble, or what they were thinking when they attempted to answer a question.

What You Can Do to Build Your Students' Understanding

Let's examine what students need to do at various points in a text to develop understanding. And remember, as a mature reader, many of these processes happen automatically for you. But for children, they don't. It often takes hard work, and understanding may not flow so easily for them.

The examples in this section are snippets of lessons designed to show you the complexities of digesting the textbase for young readers and putting it to work to build comprehension. We hope they show you the powerful diagnostic value of questions that allow you to see what students are—and are not—picking up.

Grade 3: "The Fisherman and His Wife" by The Brothers Grimm

"The Fisherman and His Wife" is the story of a fisherman's wife who discovers that her husband caught and freed a magical wish-granting fish. At this point, the couple has already been granted a cozy cottage by the fish.

"I should like very much to live in a large stone castle; so go to your fish and he will send us a castle."... The man felt very reluctant and unwilling; and he said to himself, "It is not the right thing to do;" nevertheless, he went (p. 1)....

"Husband, get up and just look out of the window. Look, just think if we could be king over all this country. Just go to your fish and tell him we should like to be king."

So the man went, very much put out that his wife should want to be king. "It is not the right thing to do—not at all the right thing," thought the man.

He did not at all want to go, and yet he went all the same (p. 2).

To understand the wife's progression of desires, students need to start by connecting the "large stone castle" to their relevant knowledge that a castle is a home for kings—that is, of course, if they have that knowledge. If they don't, that passage will make little sense, and the textbase can break down. Similarly, the phrase "all the same" will mean little if students don't process "The man felt reluctant and unwilling and yet," "it's not the right thing to do," and "nevertheless, he went." Students need to absorb those propositions to understand not only the meaning of "he went all the same," but also the thread of the storyline and the fisherman as a character. We build larger understandings by integrating propositions seamlessly. Some readers may do that automatically, but it can take effort even for proficient readers—and even more for English learners who may not be familiar with the nuances and syntax of English.

We need to ask questions that help students make the connections necessary to form a valid textbase. We believe questions are helpful if they are deliberately designed to be so. A good question will send students right back into the text to discover the answer. That answer will help them understand the ideas in the text, how those ideas relate to one another, and activate relevant content knowledge. Here are some example questions for "The Fisherman and His Wife":

- Did the fisherman's wife say she wanted to be a king? If not, what did she say that made the fisherman know that's what she wanted? Explain how you know.
- Did the fisherman want to ask the fish for a castle? How do you know?

> We believe questions are helpful if they are deliberately designed to be so. A good question will send students right back into the text to discover the answer.

- The text says, "he went all the same." What does "all the same" mean? What in the text made you know this?
- What is your opinion of the fisherman after reading this part? Tell what words or phrases helped you form your opinion.

This Q&A could happen with the whole class, or in pairs or small groups, after students have had a chance to think individually. We prefer larger group discussions because they give all students access to the thinking of their classmates and provide constant feedback to the teacher on who is easily making connections and who isn't. It's also a lot more fun. You can save written responses for questions that require more reflection before discussing them. That approach can generate thoughtful exchanges. But we recommend they come after all the students have had a chance to make these connections and build at least an accurate textbase and basic situation model of the story as a whole.

Students explaining their thinking.

Those types of questions help students understand the text's propositions and make connections among them and to relevant content knowledge. Doing all that helped them develop their textbase for the story. Some students will be able to answer these questions effortlessly, which tells you they made those connections and have the relevant content knowledge. Other students may have to stop and think before making connections, but with effort, they will. And other students will be stymied because they don't understand the propositions. That could possibly be because of the unfamiliar language (e.g., "I should like very much," "reluctant," "unwilling," and "not the right thing"), or they weren't able to connect the propositions to one another. Perhaps they didn't have the relevant content knowledge—or they did have it but, for some reason, failed to activate it because they didn't yet have a strong Standard of Coherence.

Let's look at other text excerpts and what they demand at various grade levels.

Grade 6: *The Great Fire* by Jim Murphy

Consider the first paragraph from Jim Murphy's *The Great Fire* about the Chicago fire of 1871:

> It was Sunday and an unusually warm evening for October eighth, so Daniel "Peg Leg" Sullivan left his stifling little house in the west side of Chicago and went to visit neighbors. One of his stops was at the shingled cottage of Patrick and Catherine O'Leary. The one-legged Sullivan remembered getting to the O'Learys' house at around eight o'clock, but left after only a few minutes because the O'Leary family was already in bed. Both Patrick and Catherine had to be up very early in the morning: he to set off for his job as a laborer; she to milk their five cows and then deliver the milk to the neighbors.

To understand what follows and why Mrs. O'Leary and her cow are so famous, students would need to recognize that "the O'Learys" are the same as "Patrick and Catherine," and that they go to bed early because they have to get up early to milk cows.

This paragraph also contains a nice example of how a proposition later in the text—in this case, "one-legged"—can spark learning of something earlier in the text—the meaning of "Peg Leg."

Here are some possible questions to ask students to answer and explain:

- Who had to go to bed early?
- Why did they have to go to bed early?
- Who is "Peg Leg" and why do you think he got that name?

Because students will know from its title that the book is about a fire, you could also ask, "Why do you think the author included details, such as their 'shingled cottage' and 'one-legged Sullivan'?" Students *might* infer that shingles were the kind made of wood so they would burn easily, and that someone with one leg *might* have trouble escaping a fire. Clearly, not every student will have such intuition. Many of them might not know what shingles are and, if they do, that they're made of wood. But raising questions like that calls attention to the importance of a text's details. You never know the subtle inferences and insights students have, and you won't find out unless you ask them questions that require a high level of thinking and analysis.

Grade 5: *Esperanza Rising* by Pam Muñoz Ryan

Here's another example, for upper elementary, from *Esperanza Rising* by Pam Muñoz Ryan. Here, we're showing you how a situation model forms in parallel with the reader forming a textbase understanding. Remember, the *situation model* is a reader's deeper sense of what the text means, a sense that's continually adjusting as more of the text is read. The textbase develops from the reader working to parse meaning proposition by proposition. Both are essential to comprehension.

Here's a situation model: Esperanza is almost 13. She's had an idyllic life as the child of a wealthy grape grower. But her father has been murdered by his stepbrothers who have also burned down her family home to drive her mother and her out. The privileged life Esperanza had known is dissolving. She and her mother are fleeing to California. Here, Abuelita, Esperanza's grandmother, is giving her a dose of courage:

> Abuelita squeezed Esperanza's hand. "Do not be afraid to start over. When I was your age, I left Spain with my mother, father, and sisters. A Mexican official had offered my father a job here in Mexico. So we came. We had to take several ships and the journey lasted months. When we arrived, nothing was as promised. There were many hard times. But life was also exciting." (p. 49)

Abuelita does this by telling the story of how her own family had immigrated to Mexico from Spain. That's the addition to the situation model from *this* passage.

For a student reader to arrive at that, he or she would need to integrate these propositions in the passage:

1. Abuelita comforts Esperanza (by squeezing her hand).

2. She tells her not to be afraid.

3. Esperanza is on the verge of starting over.

4. Abuelita was Esperanza's age when the events in her own story happened.

5. She, too, had to relocate to an unknown place.

6. A Mexican government person offered her father a job.

7. Abuelita and her family had to relocate from Spain to Mexico. (Students must infer that the family moved because of the job offer.)

8. It was a hard journey.

9. When they arrived, there was no job or anything else that had been promised.

10. That made life difficult.

11. But there were exciting parts to the new life, too.

There is more cognitive work for students to do. ("A Mexican official had offered my father a job." But when they arrived after a difficult journey, "nothing was as promised.") Students need to infer that the second phrase points back to the job offer and parse that phrase "nothing was as promised" to realize the job didn't materialize and that created hardship. Many students may not know the expression "as promised." But most would know "promise," so if they connect that knowledge to "nothing was as promised," they will comprehend what is happening here and learn a new expression.

Students must string those propositions together to form a textbase and to update their situation model. They need to parse an expression they might not have seen before. Also, a text like this will resonate differently with students if they recall something related from their knowledge or experience. Some readers may themselves have made a perilous journey from elsewhere to start over in a new place. Different students might form successful textbase understandings but develop different situation models based on their knowledge and even their own feelings about what Esperanza is going through.

Remember, all these processes are going on at once. The reader is processing and developing the surface level through fluent word-level reading. He or she is processing and understanding vocabulary even as he or she is forming the textbase, by connecting propositions and activating relevant knowledge. All that cognitive work feeds the formation of the situation model. Reading is amazing!

Grade 2: *Owen & Mzee: The True Story of a Remarkable Friendship* by Isabella Hatkoff, Craig Hatkoff, and Paula Kahumbu

Read-alouds can and should happen even before students can read independently. If you've ever read to preschoolers, you know how closely they attend to the book even though they are unable to read it themselves. They are developing a textbase and a situation model aurally. While they aren't engaging with the surface level of the text (meaning, decoding for themselves), if they can see the text as they listen to it, they are absorbing some of that foundational skills knowledge. But that is not the focus of this section. Instead, we're going to focus on developing listening comprehension, which grows vocabulary, knowledge, and familiarity with different types of texts.

This is the true story of a baby hippo stranded on a reef during a tsunami. His pod was lost, so he's an orphan, too young to take care of himself. After being rescued by local villagers, Owen was taken to an animal sanctuary. There, the lonely hippo was befriended by a 130-year-old tortoise, Mzee. The pair became famous worldwide for their loyal friendship. Scientists had never seen this sort of interspecies friendship before.

This passage takes place shortly after Owen was placed with Mzee, but was not yet eating.

At first, Owen wouldn't eat any of the leaves left out for him. Stephen and the other caretakers were worried that he would weaken even more. Then they noticed Owen feeding right beside Mzee, as if Mzee were showing him how to eat. Or perhaps it was Mzee's protective presence that helped Owen feel calm enough to eat. No one will ever know. But it was clear that the bond between Owen and Mzee was helping the baby hippo to recover from being separated from his mother and stranded in the sea.

With Mzee by his side, Owen began to eat.

Key question: What did the authors mean by "No one will ever know"?

To answer that question, first students would need to have absorbed all the information about Owen starting to eat and the fact that he was eating alongside Mzee. They would then need to understand that this one short sentence containing a single proposition connects to and references multiple propositions about Owen's failure to eat that came before the sentence. They need to understand how weak Owen was from not eating and infer how worried the caretakers were that Owen wasn't going to eat at all and might die.

But that is only the first part of what students would need to understand about what won't ever be known. They would also need to understand what this means when the authors say, "No one will ever know." This contrasts with several earlier places in the book where scientists *did* know things about hippo and tortoise behavior to show that this is an important part of science: There are things we know and things we don't. That question also acts as a preview of the final page of the story where the unknowns about why these two are such buddies are addressed in more detail.

Students have to do a lot of work to connect propositions before they can understand the victory of Owen starting to eat and the mystery of what caused the breakthrough. *At first* he wouldn't eat. The caretakers *were worried. Then they noticed* [that Owen was eating]. *As if Mzee was showing him how. Or perhaps* [he now felt safer so he could eat]. After the acknowledgment that we won't ever be sure, the text continues with: *But it was clear* [the connection between them] *was helping the baby hippo recover.*

As if and *or perhaps* are both connectives that convey uncertainty in this passage, and students may not recognize the role they play. Then they see *But*, which usually conveys the opposite of something. Here it is being used to convey certainty (*it was clear*), as opposed to what wasn't clear earlier. Students need to toggle in their understanding of what isn't known to what is in the span of these three sentences.

The vocabulary second graders may not know are all concrete words: *protective, presence, recover,* and *stranded* that could be dropped in during the first read.

No matter what grade, it is powerful to engage students in this process of responding to questions about a carefully selected section of text. When you couple that with asking students to explain what they were thinking to arrive at a response, you are doing what you need to do to build reading comprehension.

Unfortunately, this research-based, intellectually satisfying process is rare. Instead, we ask students to spend their time doing things that have little to no research base for building comprehension.

The Hazards of a Single Focus on Reading Strategies

It's been common practice for decades to provide students with a bucketful of tools in the form of strategies to grow their reading comprehension (for example, a lesson focused on finding the main idea/key details or making predictions). Unfortunately, it doesn't work. Let's look at why.

It's Not the Way We Read

Here's the big reason looking for one construct at a time is problematic: It's simply not the way proficient readers approach or absorb a text.

We've spent a lot of time convincing you that reading is a coherent series of processes that happen all at once. Those processes reinforce one another and support successful reading comprehension.

This practice does the opposite, muddying what reading comprehension is by oversimplifying and isolating a single component of it. Often this means building lessons around focus standards and reading only for mastery of that standard. The idea is that if students truly understand a standard, they will be able to answer questions that map to that standard, and repetition of this for standard after standard will make them stronger readers. This misguided belief, again, baked deeply into our instructional materials, programs, and assessments, is that this ability will transfer to other texts. It doesn't.

As we've been saying, there could be any number of reasons why the student gets a question wrong (or doesn't understand what's happening in the text) other than not understanding the standard. In fact, it's highly probable there's something else going on, and you won't know what if you aren't focused on the interchange between the confused student and the text.

Two Examples of Missed Opportunities

David was observing a middle school class reading a junior version of *Oedipus Rex*, the great tragedy by Sophocles. The class read a section where the Greek chorus said something to the effect that it takes a lifetime to know if a man is good but an evil man can be spotted in a moment ("You'll learn this well, without fail, in time/Time alone can bring the just man to light/The criminal you can spot in one short day." Lines 688–690).

David stopped following along and pondered what he thought was an extremely interesting notion. He observed a number of the students felt the same way. It turned out the lesson did not include a question addressing this point because it did not relate to the standard for that week. So the teacher moved right on.

Another time, David was observing a kindergarten class during read-aloud. When the teacher finished each page, she would stop and have students "ask a question," "make an inference," "visualize," whichever was the comprehension strategy(ies) being addressed that week or day. They would then go on to the next page and do the same. *All of this* was during initial reading of the text before finishing the book.

Neither teacher was at fault. Their curriculum materials directed them to ask students to read for one particular construct.

But It's What Weak Readers Do

We've seen this operate tragically in leveled-reading approaches. A mentor text is read aloud addressing a single standard or literary element. It fits. It's really there in the mentor text, which invariably is rich and complex at grade level. But students are then asked to hunt in their own leveled texts for examples of this. It might not even be there. Or the texts may be too simple to contain such an element at the same level of sophistication (which often happens) or be in a place where that standard could operate meaningfully. We don't want reading itself to feel absurd to children, *ever*.

But here's the heart of the tragedy: What we've continually observed is that proficient readers essentially ignore this directive. They might scan and find the thing in case they're held accountable. What they're mostly doing is reading for meaning because that's what proficient readers do all the time.

But weaker readers, who are accustomed to not understanding what they read at any level and generally not confident about their reading, grab onto this single focus as a lifeline. "Oh, I don't have to struggle to understand this text. All I need to do is hunt for an example of this one construct I was asked to read for!" In essence, this approach is teaching weak readers how *not* to read.

It Doesn't Align With the Science of Comprehension

Our thinking about strategies is heavily influenced by the study by McKeown et al. (2009).

Over two years, in fifth-grade classrooms, McKeown et al. (2009) researched three methods of teaching comprehension that emphasized discussion:

1. A traditional basal, already in use in the district

2. A comprehension-strategies approach

3. A "content approach," in which the researchers asked questions centered on readings, along the lines of "Why did this happen?"; "What do you think this means?"; and "What is he saying here?". We call this asking text-dependent questions. In this third method, when students were confused, the researchers encouraged them to refer to the text. This approach was much like what we've been arguing for.

Here's a summary of the results from the study:

- In the content approach, students talked for longer and their talk centered on what they'd read. This enabled students to remember more of what they'd read.

- Strategies prompts generally shifted students away from talking about content to talking about use of strategies.

- By taking them first through the strategy routine, a strategies focus led students to consider what they'd read more indirectly, through the lens of the strategy.

- Questions asked in the content lessons, on the other hand, encouraged students to express and integrate what they had understood from what they'd read.

McKeown et al. (2009) also recommend "that at least some of the time teachers work through a text with students alternating reading with discussion," which is what we recommend. They pointed out the teacher benefits from this format "in being able to observe confusion as it occurs and consider what the source of the confusion might be."

McKeown et al. (2009) came to call the third method from their research "questioning the author."

What Is the Role of Strategies?

We do believe there's a role for comprehension strategies. But it's a limited one, and the use of strategies should be more organic than is currently the case.

Based on the research gathered by Tim Shanahan (2016), the most effective strategies are:

- comprehension monitoring (noticing when you don't understand and going back to figure out why).
- stopping and summarizing while reading.
- asking questions of the text while reading.
- using text structure as an aid.

As Dan Willingham (2006) noted, strategies are easy and quick to learn, but it's important to remember the point of learning them.

In the question-based approach we've been arguing for, students might use those strategies to explain their thinking behind a response to a question, often without naming the strategy. When their understanding breaks down, we can shift the conversation back to the text by asking questions that encourage strategy use: "What could you have done to figure that out?" or "Can you explain where your understanding broke down?" Again, the goal here is for students to transfer this self-questioning and self-explaining to their independent reading all the time. Then these tools will have become their own. That's what we mean by an organic approach to folding these few strategies into classroom discourse.

In sum, working with a strategies- or standards-first approach detours students' attention. It removes them from what they're reading and requires them to take a second step to answer a question or figure out what's happening, instead of focusing directly on the text. In the study we just looked at, when students struggled with a question, the teacher would ask them to use a strategy, and the students would get tongue-tied trying to determine which strategy to use. They wandered far off the text. It's awfully hard to comprehend a text when you're assigned tasks that distract you from it.

It's awfully hard to comprehend a text when you're assigned tasks that distract you from it.

We believe the best place to teach and reinforce strategies in moderation is when you're setting expectations for independent reading—where students read the volume that will grow their knowledge of words and the world. Brief lessons regarding what to do when understanding breaks will cement these learnings. This aligns with psychologist Dan Willingham's stance: "Strategies are learned quickly, and continued instruction and practice does not yield further benefits" (Willingham, 2006/2007).

All of this doesn't mean we should stop asking *any* questions addressing standards. We know that's unrealistic in our current climate. And we believe it's worthwhile to have standards as targets for end-of-year mastery. In Chapter 7, we'll show you how to tuck them in without letting them dominate instruction. Rather, it's the drive to make meaning from text that should come first and dominate.

In Closing, Remember...

- Each text is essentially a frozen kaleidoscope, presenting its own combination of features and its own unique degree of challenge.
- Features of text can combine in numerous ways to create obstacles to comprehension.
- What's most important in helping students comprehend complex text is to teach ourselves to notice and focus on the most challenging parts of that text.
- Our primary goal should always be to help students comprehend text. Everything else (e.g., strategies, standards) should be in service of comprehension.
- Consistently asking students to explain their thinking using evidence from the text is the way to "peek inside their minds" and see what they misunderstood.
- In general, students should have a chance to address text-dependent questions individually before any pair or group work.
- Pair or group work is essential to developing language and especially helpful for multilingual learners.
- Focusing on any one feature/strategy/standard at a time is not helpful as the complexity and challenge are formed by the interactions of the features.

In the next chapter, we zero in on close reading and all that it can do to cultivate comprehension. Because asking questions is such a crucial part of the close-reading process, we'll teach you more about how to craft well-directed questions to support student understanding of complex text.

The Power of Close Reading

The outcome of successful, proficient reading is comprehension, delivered in the form of a solid situation model. It's common to view comprehension as a single process, as we ourselves did for years. But, as we hope we've made clear, it's made up of a variety of processes that come together simultaneously and repeatedly build on one another while reading.

We promised in the introduction that we'd reveal how to "see inside your students' minds" to understand what they are thinking and identify where they're having trouble with comprehension. It's time for that reveal.

Students and teachers engaging in those processes is key to building reading comprehension for all. In fact, it's the missing ingredient in the science of reading.[3] And close reading is the best context we know for this regular engagement in the work of improving reading comprehension.

---

[3] The science-of-reading community has been vital to getting early reading instruction on track with rock-solid research, but its laser focus on foundational skills has led too many people to conclude that those skills (and sometimes knowledge) are all there is to reading.

You might have a sense of close reading from your own work. We've certainly been alluding to it in earlier portions of the book—particularly in Chapter 6 with our emphasis on questions and the value of self-explanation. Here's our definition: Close reading is when students are attending carefully to a text, reading it several times, each for a different purpose, and mining it for all they possibly can, while you are close by, observing, facilitating, and coaching as needed.

We want to be clear that there is absolutely no research-based "best way" to do it. That question hasn't even been investigated, let alone settled. The steps and processes we're presenting incorporate all the research-based best practices we've explored throughout the book. And we've seen that key parts of this process, such as providing proof of your answer, worked well for the students we've worked closest with over the years. So, flex your previous notions of close reading as you continue reading. That way, you'll see the potency of the moves we're advocating and then make a system that will work for you and your students.

Close Reading Is for All Students

Close reading is for all students, regardless of their reading ability or facility with English. It can support every reader in your classroom. All kids deserve access to rich, grade-level text. We haven't yet come across any other approach that provides both this level of opportunity and support-as-needed for all students to engage regularly with grade-level text.

Here's why: Answering questions that focus on the text provides a pathway to comprehension. What reading for comprehension looks like is made clear. Providing evidence by explaining your answers is hard intellectual work. It's often a challenge for even highly competent readers to engage in this kind of metacognition regularly.

Close reading provides robust support for students reading below, and even well below, grade level. But that support needs to be deliberately built in. It must be designed for native English speakers, students just learning English, and everyone in between. We've yet to find a better, more consistent way to support all those students to read grade-level text. In the next section we suggest supports that teachers we worked with have found extremely helpful. We hope you do, too!

Our System for Close Reading

In spite of all the positive things we did at the Family Academy, we noticed too many students were reading grade-level texts independently but missing important points. Though the knowledge and vocabulary demands didn't always seem significant, a fair number of students would get quite a few of the questions we posed to them wrong. Because going straight to the source is one of David's favorite research methods, he asked a group of fourth-grade students he was working with what they should do if they get a question wrong. The unanimous answer was, "Read that section again." So, they did. When he asked them some of the same questions again, some of their answers were still wrong. When David asked them again what they should do, they responded, "Read it again!" After several failed do-overs, our students were getting understandably restless. Then Henry Dixon, a quiet, thoughtful kid (now working for Apple), said, "Mr. Liben, there has to be some other way."

Henry was onto something. In fact, this whole exercise was a bit of a setup to gain student buy-in. We'd already been working with faculty members to address the high-error patterns on texts we believed our students were capable of reading with full comprehension. We called our close-reading system "Textual Analysis."

Initially, our goal was to make sure all our students could confidently navigate the high-stakes state tests we had performed so grimly on early in the school's life. But it soon became the intellectual nucleus of everyone's school day. Students got so good at closely reading text and especially at explaining their findings, they used to intimidate teachers new to the school and the idea of reading that closely for meaning.

Our understanding of what's optimal for comprehension instruction has evolved over the years. But it still revolves around a simple, sustainable system for close reading. What we're sharing with you has been informed by:

- Our years of experience at the Family Academy, doing close reading 45 to 50 minutes a day, four days a week, throughout the year, in Grades 3–8.
- Absorbing the research on how the mind comprehends text that we've shared in Chapter 5.
- The work we've done with Student Achievement Partners and schools throughout the country since 2010, with the introduction of College and Career Readiness standards and the Common Core State Standards, *especially* the demand that requires that students comprehend grade-level texts.
- The feedback and amazing ideas we've gotten over the years from teachers and students.

Many approaches to close reading we've seen are too complicated and have lots of moving parts and supplements. Our approach is simple. Our perspective is that teaching is demanding and complex and becoming more so. We taught close reading to students for years and we've also taught a lot of teachers how to teach it. In the process, we've learned that a simpler system is more likely to be successful over the long haul. It's also easier to implement, whether you have a comprehensive ELA program that includes many of the practices or not.

Our system of course starts with the teacher reading the text prior to working with students and carefully selecting or creating a few questions that focus on the features of the text most likely to cause difficulty. Then the class spends some time each day for a few days (generally 3 or 4 chunks of 30 to 45 minutes) on the text selection, reading the text a total of three times, each time with a different purpose.

If you've never taught close reading, there's a learning curve. Don't be hard on yourself or feel you have to do every step exactly as we explain it. You and your students will get better with practice. And if you stay the course, your students will amaze you daily with their reading prowess.

Before the Close-Reading Lesson

Preparing for close reading is essential. There are no shortcuts. First and foremost, read the text closely yourself so you can anticipate where your students might run into trouble and see what's most important and interesting.

Text Selection: Text Worth Reading

When it comes to text selection, you need to be picky. If the text isn't worth reading, don't use it. Find one that is worth reading.

Close reading can be done with any grade-level text,[4] whether it's from a program you are using or one you've selected. Try to pick a text that won't take more than a week at most to read deeply and reflect upon in a culminating assignment. Short poems or rich paragraphs will work well for briefer close-reading lessons. If you're reading a full-length book as a class, select passages that are crucial to the book's development and to your teaching goals for the book. Try to pick passages you think are complex, are of particular importance, or beautifully written.

Text Preparation: Work Worth Doing

Everything you do should engage your students in one of the interconnected ingredients of comprehension we've looked at so far. What follows are snapshots of those ingredients and how to fold them into your close-reading lessons.

TEXTBASE PREP

Carefully read the text you're planning to use. Highlight and/or annotate parts you think may be difficult for many students; and note vocabulary, concepts, and references you suspect will be new to students. Think about the big understanding you want students to gain from the reading. Also think about the culminating writing or other creative task you will ask students to do to demonstrate that understanding. We talk about the value of doing extended writing both for its own sake and for cementing comprehension in Chapter 8. This kind of "backward design" thinking will influence the questions you ask during the lesson.

---

[4] Grade-level text complexity usually is measured by the three-part system developed for college and career readiness standards. (We led this work for the Common Core State Standards, and it is still the accepted measure.)

VOCABULARY PREP

Grade-level complex text will inevitably contain vocabulary students do not know and likely won't be able to define using context. So reread the text, this time looking for words worthy of studying in depth. They might include:

- More abstract words
- Words students are likely to see in other contexts and grade levels
- Words that are part of a family or network of words (e.g., *action*, *actionable*, *active*, *activation*)

Make a list of the words you selected and create a question about each word that will draw students' attention to it and spark discussion to develop vocabulary depth.

Then look for concrete, easy-to-define words students will need to understand the passage but might not know. These are your "drop-in words" as you'll drop in the word's meaning during the first reading of the passage with students. See Chapter 2, page 50, for more information on drop-in words.

SYNTAX PREP

Read the text one more time to note any particularly "juicy sentences" you think are worth exploring more in depth. You can explore them deeply during the third read. Read about juicy sentences in Chapter 8, page 140.

KNOWLEDGE-BUILDING PREP

Avoid or minimize pre-teaching what the text is about. Even from the beginning of a fictional narrative, readers will develop an initial sense of what the text is about (a budding situation model) that will evolve as they continue reading. If you provide too much information up front, students won't learn how to do that for themselves and it's a crucial behavior for them to develop. In short, do your best to wait for students to signal you before rushing in to fill a knowledge gap.

The possible exception may be with English learners who may have little framework or context for what they're encountering in the text. Even then, find a short video or a simpler text to build requisite knowledge for these students, if you can, and do this before the rest of the class begins work with the text. This boosts confidence without taking away the opportunity to work on the grade-level text with everyone else.

See what we've done thus far in this chapter? All the information in Chapters 1–6 has been rolled up, taught, expanded, and strengthened in your students' minds, each and every time you do close reading of rich, grade-level text. That's why close reading is so effective.

> ### Text Sets as Powerful Knowledge Supports
>
> Text sets, which we describe in Chapter 1, are great scaffolds for developing Tier 2 vocabulary and content knowledge that students can use when they read complex texts closely. Text sets also teach students to use what they learn from reading to learn more. When they can apply that to reading complex texts closely, it's a great reinforcer.

Watch David and Meredith interview teachers about effective close-reading tips.

During the Close-Reading Lesson

For the lesson, you'll do three separate reads of the same text for different instructional purposes, most likely over a few days. Longer texts can be broken into chunks after an initial read, as discussed below. Multiple reads of the text for different purposes are in themselves one of the best supports for students, especially striving students. After you've read the text multiple times with a different focus and purpose each time, you can give students a culminating assignment so they can see for themselves how much they've learned. We'll break each reading down into more detail next.

The First Read

Read the text aloud while students follow along, stopping only to explain words you've identified as essential to understanding the content and likely to be unfamiliar to most kids. Some will be drop-in words (as explained in Chapter 2, page 50); others might be words you return to later for more time and attention. This unencumbered first read, with students following along in their own copies, will help bring your striving readers and English learners into the text.

Starting this way will have substantial positive effects on student fluency if it becomes a regular part of instruction (LaBerge & Samuels, 1974; Samuels, 1979; Lee & Yoon, 2017; Dohower, 1987; Chomsky, 2002; Brown et al., 2017). If you're confident one or more of your students can read aloud with expression instead of or in addition to you, that's a plus. Invite them to read!

After the first read, have students write a gist statement of what this text is about. Then ask them to jot any questions, thoughts, or wonderings they have about what was read. The writing shouldn't be lengthy. The idea is for students to capture their initial responses and for you to know if anyone is lost at this early point so you can offer support. You can have a quick discussion instead of writing to collectively form the gist as long as you can monitor for individuals who still aren't getting the gist.

Revisiting the Standard of Coherence

Gaining a high Standard of Coherence is a natural outcome of daily close reading, especially if students are expected to explain their thinking. Remember, a high Standard of Coherence is a habit of mind that expects what you read to make sense and to do something about it when it doesn't. See Chapter 5, page 89, for more information.

Habits can be cultivated.

Most young people in our country learn to read and grow as readers during school. This habit of mind can be an outgrowth of how we teach students to read for understanding, for it is in school they develop beliefs about themselves as readers. We need to help them develop the belief that they can understand what they read if they work at it, are encouraged, and shown how.

To develop a strong Standard of Coherence, we need to present students with texts that challenge them. Then we need to present them with text-related tasks that give them a chance to respond on their own or with peers, and then to affirm or refine those responses with teacher feedback (Oudega & van den Broek, 2018), which is the ultimate goal of a good close-reading lesson. That's *exactly* what will be going on during the second read.

Students who are investigating rich, complex text on a regular basis are building up their reading muscles and stamina. When they're encouraged (required!) to explain their thinking regarding what the text is communicating, they're constantly refining their ability to read carefully. With your encouragement and the good questions you'll be asking during the second read, students learn not to back away from working to comprehend the text.

This second read is really where much of the crucial work of close reading happens for students.

That's the plan. Let's see how to make it happen.

The All-Important Second Read

It's all about the questions. The idea here is to pose several mighty questions that guide students to the thinking necessary to overcome what makes the passage challenging. We've prepared the tip box on the following page to help you.

Don't worry. Sometimes there's so much going on in text, you'll miss something. And you won't ever be able to ask everything you want. Depending on how much time you have and the length of the text, you may have to just prepare 4–7 good questions. But your students will still be learning how to read more deeply and will start to notice these features of text and how they combine to present obstacles for themselves. Eventually, they'll do that even when you haven't asked a question about a given section.

When students explain their thinking—as they always must—it makes visible to everyone how the section you're discussing contributes to the text's meaning, why it presented a challenge, and how that challenge can be navigated. Through students explaining their thinking, you are, in essence, building a collective understanding of how to put all the components of reading comprehension together to arrive at an accurate understanding. While learning about the world, they're learning about reading, itself.

Students should first address questions independently before addressing them in pairs or small groups, to give them a chance to make sense of the text on their own. It can be motivating and give students and you a sense of what questions are most difficult. Be careful not to leave students lacking in skills and confidence on their own for too long; they may shut down if they're faced with solo work they can't do. You need to know which students would benefit from a buddy system right away, rather than working alone so they can process meaning orally with a partner.

Tips for Preparing Mighty Questions

Prepare questions that focus on the toughest and/or most important sections of the text. If you're using an ELA program, preview and replace questions and tasks that don't do those two things. Think about the following potential obstacles to comprehension when coming up with questions:

- Lack of sentences or paragraphs that review, summarize, or connect propositions across the text
- Longer paragraphs
- Short paragraphs
- A text structure that is less narrative and/or mixes structures
- Subtle and/or frequent transitions
- Concepts and ideas that are implied, but not stated
- Multiple and/or subtle themes and purposes
- Density of information
- Unfamiliar settings, topics, or events
- Lack of repetition, few connectives, or overlap between propositions
- Complex sentences (these often contain multiple propositions)
- Less common or even obscure vocabulary
- Pronoun references. These can be hard, and especially when they pile up, many students find them hard to trace back to their antecedents. This can happen a lot with dialogue and is a particular challenge for English learners.

- Words that change the direction the reader thought he or she was moving in. Students can easily skip over words such as *but*, *however*, *or*, and *not*, and lose the thread as a result. We told our students when they were doing close reading (in any subject) to circle "not." David remembers when one fourth grader learning to read closely was rereading the text. David called on him to explain his answer, and, suddenly realizing he failed to incorporate "not" into his analysis, the student yelled out, "Dang, Mr. Liben! Those small words can kill you!"

The presence or absence of those potential obstacles will vary from text to text, but over time you will learn to recognize them easily and focus on those that will challenge your students.

Those features interact, often in ways that support comprehension. A subtle transition may not be so difficult if its importance is signaled with words or phrases; some words you think many students might not know may be well supported by surrounding text; a necessary connection to an earlier proposition may be supported with words that cue the student. As you've learned, there are a limited number of text features that can present obstacles to comprehension but a far larger number of ways they can combine.

BUT WHERE DO THE STANDARDS COME IN?

We understand the frustration behind questions like this one. After all, educators at every level are held accountable for how students do on standards-based assessments annually. The short answer is, there is room for them in close reading, and it's during the third read. The truth is, standards need to be mastered by the end of the school year, *not* the end of a lesson. The ELA College and Career Readiness standards are designed to be annual targets. They're an agreed-upon set of expectations for what students should know about and be able to do with grade-level text, at the end of each grade. The idea is to put students on track for success by the time they finish high school and can move on to their desired next steps with minimum fuss.

Standards in all the ELA strands (not just the reading strands) should, of course, be considered in curriculum planning, reflected in instructional materials, and kept in mind for all students. But our primary goal should be helping students to understand texts and to express that understanding in insightful discussions and writing. If students don't understand the text, they cannot address a standards-based question, either in instruction or assessment. If they *can* comprehend grade-level texts, they stand a much better chance of attaining annual standards of achievement.

In sum, the questions we ask about complex texts and activities we do need to focus not only on students demonstrating understanding, but also on what might be blocking their comprehension so they can learn to comprehend even when it's a challenge. That needs to be the major focus of the work that happens during the second read.

If You're Using a Core Reading Program...

If you're using a high-quality ELA program, you may already be doing a lot of what we're describing. The Knowledge Matters Campaign curates and displays these programs. If you're using a traditional basal program, please follow our guidelines closely. Your materials may center around reading strategies or state standards during close-reading instruction instead of what actually needs to be done for your students to understand the text. Here's our guidance: If you find yourself wading through a bunch of questions and guidelines that are only marginally useful, don't use them. Instead, say our "Work Worth Doing" mantra to yourself and get rid of all that clutter!

Tips for Supporting Students During Close Reading

- If a day or two passes between the first and second read, consider having students follow along again during the second read. Or have them read the text independently or with a buddy. The configuration you choose depends on the length and complexity of the text (not all grade-level texts are equally complex) combined with your students' abilities. A third option is to read aloud with just the students who need support, having them follow along, as the rest of the class works independently.

- If you teach small groups, group students homogeneously and spend more time with the less proficient groups. This is not the same as traditional leveled reading. These students will be working with the same grade-level text as their classmates, only with more support to meet their needs. When you're working with these groups or one-on-one with students, have the other students read independently or with a buddy.

- Not every student or group will work at the same pace, so determine a good stopping point to discuss student responses and check for understanding as a class. This is important because good questions are not "gotchas." They are designed to support comprehension.

- Find times to work with struggling students before the rest of the class does the initial reading as often as you can. Give them a preview reading. If you can't, coordinate with an intervention teacher to do it. Not only does this give kids who need it a leg up when it comes to comprehending the text, it also boosts multilingual students, too, of course.

- In either case, when providing an additional oral reading, encourage students to address something more specific and different after their second read by asking them questions such as, "Did you have any new questions?"; "Were any earlier questions answered for you?"; "Is this text similar to any other texts we have read this year?"; or "Was there something that surprised you?"

- When students are answering questions in pairs or small groups, match them up linguistically so they can discuss questions and the text in their home language before they present their thoughts to the whole class in English.

The Third Read

The third read offers a lot of latitude, depending on what you chose as the meatiest parts of the text during preparation. You may want to focus on a juicy sentence and unpack it, using the juicy sentence protocol you'll learn about in Chapter 8. You may want to direct students' attention to those high-value vocabulary words worth spending time on; perhaps unpacking the morphemes within them. You may want to ask some questions based on the reading, listening, and/or language standards that you think fit with the text. Is character development paramount in the text? Ask questions about the characters. Is the sequence of events crucial to grasp? Focus students' attention there. Does it make sense to examine the author's purpose for writing the text? Ditto.

There might also be an additional opportunity to grow knowledge from the text, so you could ask questions that help students learn new information from their close reading. Remember, this should *not* be your primary way to grow knowledge. Increasing your students' volume of reading should be. See Chapter 1 for more on that. But if time allows, why not, as Meredith's mother used to say, "Seize the opportunity for the acquisition of further knowledge"?

You can also check the questions you've already asked to see what standards they cover. Remember—you don't have to address every standard while closely reading a text. In doing close reading over the course of the year, you will have numerous opportunities to address all the standards, and give your students practice in them. They will arise organically from the rich texts you're exposing your students to, week after week. If you are using grade-level text, you'll be addressing the Common Core State Standards' text complexity standard[5] with every text you use for close reading. And if you're asking students to explain the thinking behind their answers to each question you ask, you're pulling into the lesson that all-important evidence standard, along with applying the robust research on the power of self-explanation we discussed in Chapter 6. And guess what? You're teaching your students to read for meaning at grade level. And isn't that the point?

After the Close-Reading Lesson

We recommend thinking ahead of time about what you want students to come away with from the lesson, and creative ways for students to express what they've learned.

Culminating Assignment: Learning Worth Remembering

A culminating assignment is a great way to do that. The assignment needn't be elaborate, nor take much time. The goal is for students to be able to capture some enduring understanding about what they've read. This enduring understanding and the discussion around it should align well with the situation model you want students to gain from the reading. At the end of the day, it's the situation model that sticks with students and is what they'll recall of this reading experience. We touch more on the power of writing to support all this in Chapter 8.

---

[5] Since 2010, even states that developed their own college and career readiness standards have included a standard for grade-level text complexity.

Close Reading an Excerpt From Angela Cervantes's *Lety Out Loud*

In this section, we show you how to prepare a text for a close-reading lesson that touches on many aspects of comprehension. Specifically, we present a dialogue between us, in which David makes observations and poses questions as he reads an excerpt from Angela Cervantes's delightful *Lety Out Loud,* and Meredith responds with implications for a close-reading lesson. David asks more questions than he usually would to show you as many examples of the kinds of thinking to engage in when preparing a lesson.

In the excerpt, Lety, the protagonist, is anxious about the competition she's gotten pulled into at the animal shelter while attending a summer volunteers' camp. This excerpt brings up many of the important conflicts and themes in the book.

Excerpt From Chapter 4:
"Adios, Spike"

Brisa gathered Lety and Kennedy into a huddle.

"We need big words, *chicas*," she said.

"High-school level words, for sure," Kennedy added, pulling her phone from her back pocket. "I'll google some and I can ask my big brother. He'll know…" Kennedy stopped and looked over at Lety, who was silent. "Are you okay?"

Why did the girls gather together? Students need to connect back to the previous chapter, where it mentions Hunter reads at a high school level. Not connecting to earlier parts of a text is a common source of error. Asking students to explain their answers would make very clear where a student went wrong. The other possibility is they didn't know the meaning of *huddle*. This is an example of how there is nearly always more than one possibility for student confusion.

Second-read question: Younger readers don't always make connections across chapters. This is not automatic and needs to be encouraged via questions like these.

Lety stood motionless as a rush of English words flooded her head. One word in particular stood out among them all: *doubt*.

Doubt was a word she knew well in English and Spanish. In Spanish, doubt was *duda*. Doubt had followed her all the way from Mexico to the United States. It was there on her first day of school when she couldn't understand a word the teacher said. It was there when some older boys sent her to the boys' bathroom instead of the girls' bathroom and then laughed at her every time they saw her in the hallway. She never thought she'd learn English, let alone make any friends at school. Though she did both, doubt had never left her side.

What do these two sentences tell you about what's happening? These sentences are a good example of how students have to simultaneously process many different parts of a text to form a textbase. First, they need to connect from the previous sentence that Kennedy not only noticed Lety's silence, but also knew she might be upset. That would explain why she was motionless. But students would need to know what the word *motionless* means and that often when someone is motionless, she is likely thinking deeply about something. Then they would need to know the meaning of *rush* and the phrase "flooded her head" as used in the sentence. To process the next sentence, they would need to know the meaning of *particular* as used here, the phrase *stood out*, the function of the preposition *among*, how colons work as punctuation, the role of the colon in emphasizing the importance of the word *doubt*, notice that it is in italics, and what that signifies. In two sentences, readers encounter propositions from a previous sentence, vocabulary of words and phrases, complex syntax, punctuation, and knowledge of the world. Students could lose the thread here due to any one or a combination of those factors. The only way to know is by asking them to explain their thinking using the text. This is a good example of how one part of a text can be far more complex and cause a breakdown in comprehension in what would otherwise be a simple passage.

Second-read question: Would emerge during preparatory analysis of passage—noticing the hard spots and framing a question to direct students to paying attention to it.

Empower your Spanish speakers to talk about *duda*.

What does "let alone" mean in this sentence? This is an unusual connective. It's possible to absorb this important paragraph without noticing the role the connector plays. But this is an opportunity to learn an important and subtle connective that, encountered in other texts, could present an obstacle. The idea that Lety had felt when she moved to the United States that making friends at school was even less likely than learning English is an important one for students to understand and empathize with.

Second-read question: Noticing connectives

What does "doubt had never left her side" mean? This one question does two things. First, it requires understanding the phrase "left her side"; second, whether the previous paragraph was absorbed.

Second-read question: Figurative language and character analysis

A loud commotion of barking and kids rushing to the door snapped Lety out of her daze.

"Everyone, Spike is leaving," Alma announced, holding Spike in her arms. "Come and say good-bye."

All of the kids gathered around Alma. Hunter leaned in to give Spike a quick kiss on the head. It was hard to stay mad at him when he could give Spike such a sweet kiss. As the group said their good-byes and moved on, Lety approached with Brisa and Kennedy.

"Let's make a little good-bye prayer for him. Lety, can you?" Brisa said.

"That's a good idea. Spike needs all the prayers he can get," Alma said, and handed Spike to Lety.

Lety gave Spike a gentle squeeze and closed her eyes. Brisa and Kennedy followed.

What big event snapped Lety out of her daze?
The explanation comes in the following sentence (Spike is leaving).

Instead of the more common case where earlier propositions are what allows for comprehending what follows, in THIS case, information that follows is necessary to comprehend the previous sentence and propositions. Also, this is a transition point, which, in general, can cause comprehension to break down, even with relatively simple texts.

Second-read question: Encourages Standard of Coherence/flexible meaning-making

What does Hunter do with Spike? What did this make Lety think? Use evidence from the text to explain.
There are five characters in this brief section with a lot of dialogue and interspersed in the midst of an important insight by Lety. This is an example of proposition density; a lot is happening in a short frame.

You could ask students to retell what is happening in this section, and include all the characters.

Another possibility is to ask what two important parts of the storyline are contained in this section.

Many students would see right away that Spike leaving is important to her but might miss the more subtle part about Lety's thoughts about Hunter.

Follow up by discussing how a character's internal thoughts can be just as or more important than events and dialogue.

Second-read question: Preparatory analysis of passage—noticing the potential hard spots and framing a question to direct students to paying attention to it. This section also introduces some dissonance to Lety's troubled relationship with Hunter so far.

"Dear Saint Francis, you loved all of God's creatures," Lety began. "We ask you to please watch over Spike. He is a hero that saved a baby girl. Now he is going to a foster home and we pray he will be safe, loved and fed the best —"

> If students don't know what a saint is, they would gather from reading that a saint has something to do with praying or religion. And that would be a legitimate piece of knowledge gained from reading.
>
> Students familiar with the idea of a saint from their religious background might learn that "God's creatures" are the special domain of Saint Francis.
>
> The important point here is not to give this information to students before reading, but rather to see what they can determine on their own.
>
> Optional points to raise during the third read to build knowledge and grow vocabulary

"Real *carne*!" Brisa interrupted excitedly.

"Yes, that he will have real steak," Lety added. "And please make sure he always has a toy to chew. Amen."

Lety gave Spike a kiss on his head. She wished so much he could be her dog. She wished so much that he was going home with her.

> This provides a great opportunity to work with syntax. There are really only two propositions here: Lety gave Spike a kiss and Lety desperately wished she could take Spike home. Asking students to combine that information into one sentence that conveys the same information just as strongly would support their understanding of syntax and strengthen their sentence-writing ability at once.
>
> Potential third-read activity

"I can tell already you're going to be an awesome shelter scribe," Alma said with a wink before taking Spike from her and whisking him out of the room.

> **Why did Alma wink when she spoke to Lety?**
> Students would need to connect to information earlier about the contest between Alma and Hunter. This requires connecting propositions that are far apart. But there's more. Students would have to have the knowledge that a wink sometimes communicates something the winker doesn't want to say aloud. Here, Alma is encouraging Lety by communicating she can win the contest. But she doesn't want to say that in front of the others, especially not Hunter.
>
> Second-read question

After Alma's kind words and Spike being whisked away, the room swirled with chatter and activity. Brisa and Kennedy joined the other cat heroes. Hunter and Mario were reading the animal profiles posted on the bulletin board. Still, Lety stood frozen. Spike's departure had made the contest more urgent to her. Had she really agreed to be a shelter scribe and compete with Hunter Farmer, the fifth grader who reads and writes at a high school level?

She thought back to her own words to Dr. Villalobos: *Sometimes people or pets that are not wanted can still become heroes—if we give them a chance.*

If Hunter thought he was going to splat her like an ant in this contest, she was going to prove him wrong. She owed it to the hero dog, Spike, and the hat-hating Finn, and all of the furry friends needing a forever family to squash the doubt and write profiles that were pure gold.

This is a perfect example of drop-in vocabulary. It's concrete and doesn't need any time spent on it. When something (or someone) is *whisked* away, it means it's been taken away quickly. It's a good drop-in phrase because it's concrete and represents a concept students would understand (i.e., leaving a place quickly).

Good activity while teacher is reading the chapter aloud, with students following along in their copies

What does the word *still* mean here? Again, transitions can cause obstacles. This is a transition from all the chatter and activity to Lety's private thoughts. Picking up on this is even harder as the transition is in the same paragraph. *Still* acts as a connective, helping students process the transition. Students learning how and why *still* does that would not only learn about the word as a connective, but would also see how transitions happen in all sorts of ways so they won't be thrown off by them when they occur. There is still more here: If students don't know this sense of *frozen*, it adds to the potential difficulty.

Second-read question: Noticing connectives and how they support comprehension

What is Lety thinking about in these two sentences? Some students might think Lety forgot what she agreed to. Others just might be confused by the second sentence and not realize it's not really a question but that she is again doubting herself. The connection should be made to her earlier doubts.

Second-read question: Reintroduces the theme of overcoming doubt and insecurity, and reminds readers of a main conflict in the book (the contest to write the animal profiles for adoptions)

What changes in Lety's thinking in these two paragraphs? Students need to understand that Lety herself is connecting what she said to Dr. Villalobos about Spike to her own situation. This is another example of connecting crucial ideas across the text.

Second- or third-read question: This is a crucial turning point for Lety. She may doubt herself but her love for the animals will drive her forward in spite of her doubts. Students need to understand this to conclude how determined she is and that we are at a turning point in the contest.

Much of *Lety Out Loud*'s Chapter 4 was simple to process. Only a few sections were challenging. That will generally be the case with full-length texts as well. Focus your lessons on the challenging sections. Keep in mind that because Lexile levels cover the entire book, they often obscure the fact that there are complex, rich sections all throughout the book. *Lety Out Loud* has a 720 Lexile level, which technically puts it in the Grades 2–3 band. But it doesn't belong there. It's clearly an upper-elementary book.

In Closing, Remember...

- Comprehension is the result of a number of processes that come together simultaneously while reading.
- Close reading is when students are carefully attending to a text, mining it for all they possibly can, while their teachers are close by, observing, facilitating, and coaching as needed.
- Close reading is for all students, regardless of their reading ability or facility with English. We've yet to find a better way to support all students on a regular basis to read grade-level text.
- Text-dependent questions in close reading should focus on:
    - the parts of the text that are likely to present the most difficulty.
    - the parts of the text that can grow students' knowledge.
    - the parts of the text connected to the goals of a unit or lesson.
    - *relevant* reading standards.
- When reading full-length texts, choose important and more complex parts for close reading.
- Engaging students in close reading and encouraging them to explain their answers to text-dependent questions regularly are effective ways to develop a high Standard of Coherence.
- Culminating assignments should be based on what you most want students to take away from the text.

Close reading is the most powerful way we've found to teach reading comprehension. It works for students with varying reading abilities. All students should routinely experience rich, complex text together as a class.

The method we've outlined is fully aligned with how reading comprehension is represented in the mind. It allows you to provide access to "text worth reading" with all your students on a regular basis. The sequence of repeated readings focused on a different purpose each time, along with the self-explanation students regularly engage in when providing evidence for their answers to your questions, build up reading comprehension like nothing else.

The discussion-based, social nature of this system is more intellectually rewarding for everyone. It also allows for one student's self-explanation to be expanded so that it provides learning about how to comprehend to all students. The habit of explaining how you arrived at your answers by delving back into the text is, as you'll see in our final chapter, one of the strongest practices of strong readers. We now shift our focus from oral language and rich communal learning to the deepened understanding that individuals can achieve through putting their thoughts in writing. We look at how powerful it is when students write about what they've learned and understood from their reading.

"What in the text made you think of that?"

Writing to Learn, Writing to Comprehend

We once got to host Katherine Paterson, Newbery-winning young adult author, for a weeklong residency at the Family Academy. In preparation, all students in fourth through eighth grade read her books in literature groups, with some of them devouring nearly everything she'd ever written. Robert, a seventh grader, was one of those students, unbeknownst to any of us. When it was his group's turn to work with Katherine, he asked her why the fathers in her novels were so often in danger or missing. All our jaws dropped, including Katherine's. She said she'd never thought about it and certainly hadn't ever been questioned about it. She asked Robert for some examples. He reeled off five in quick succession. After a long pause, Katherine said something like, "I'm not sure. But maybe it's because when I was very young, we were evacuated from Mainland China when the Japanese invaded [her parents were missionaries]. My father would often disappear for weeks at a time. I must have picked up on my mother's tension, but I wasn't told where he disappeared to until years later. Turns out, he was sneaking behind Japanese lines to take medical supplies to Chinese resistance fighters." She asked Robert what led him to notice this theme, and he said he loved her books and had been reading and rereading them all year, and the question just bubbled up from there.

Robert could synthesize Katherine Paterson's body of work and come up with a unique observation because he'd been taught to look for meaning—and value it—when he read. He expected to find it. He'd had five years of instruction in close reading and rich literature group discussions by the time he'd stumped Katherine. Five years of engaging in vigorous intellectual discussions about text and being held accountable by teachers for finding evidence in what he read and explaining his thoughts about what he'd read.

How do we make lots of readers like Robert? In addition to doing all the things we've discussed up to now, Robert had the chance to process what he read by writing about it on a regular basis. He preferred working on his own and developed into a powerful reflective writer. As we noted, we didn't realize he'd read so many of the Paterson books.

When students write about what they read, it cements and deepens their understanding. This chapter explores that reading-writing connection.

There's a clear obligation we keep asking you to accept in this chapter, as in all others: Give your students the key to the vault whenever you can! Two valued mentors in our work are Joey Hawkins and Diana Leddy of the Vermont Writing Collaborative, the lead authors of *Writing for Understanding*. Joey frequently says there shouldn't ever be any "gotchas" in school (Hawkins et al., 2008). Kids come to us to learn.

Writing and reading need to coexist. We cringe whenever we hear from a teacher still working in a setting that has a period for writing and a separate period for reading. No, thank you. They're too symbiotic. Speaking and writing, listening and reading. They're as linked as the breathing cycle. Speaking and writing are outputs (exhaling their thoughts, if you will); listening and reading provide inputs (inhaling new ideas).

Writing to Solidify Understanding

Using writing in conjunction with reading strengthens students' comprehension. Fordham et al. (2002) state, "Combining writing with reading enhances comprehension, because the two are reciprocal processes. Considering a topic under study and then writing about it requires deeper processing than reading alone entails."

You've probably experienced this deepening of insight and understanding for yourself, and it's invaluable to bring this experience to students as often as possible. It's satisfying to pull together the essential understandings you've gained from working hard to read something. Having a chance to name and examine that new learning in an extended piece of writing also helps strengthen students' Standard of Coherence, that expectation that what you read makes sense and the determination to do something about it when it doesn't, at first. There's nothing like writing about what you've read to see what you understand. We highly recommend the Vermont Writing Collaborative's *Writing for Understanding* for how to model and teach writing that builds these essential understandings, and develops potent writers, as well as deeper and more confident readers.

Nurturing Autonomous Readers Through Writing: Three Tools

We want students to be able to read whatever they want comfortably. At the same time, when they read, we want them to know how to track what's important and remember what's worth remembering, especially when they're being held accountable for doing so. We want to provide you with three valuable tools that will help students do that—and, in the process—begin to become truly autonomous readers.

Writing During Close Reading

Where does writing come in during close reading? Students need a lot of chances to gather their thoughts in writing. Ideally, they'd get the chance to record their thoughts before comparing notes with their classmates so they know they have to think for themselves. But sometimes they can record their thinking *after* they've talked in small groups, especially where you think your students really need the support of collective thinking. Students should be encouraged to refine their written responses and expand on them or correct them, particularly when they realize their thinking was incomplete or inaccurate. We want an environment where everyone feels safe to think, to share and to grow. No gotchas!

In short, brief writing and note-taking opportunities should be ubiquitous during close reading. That provides students and you with a written record of their journey through the texts they read.

The Structured Journal

When David first started teaching history at the Community College of Vermont, he knew that a three-hour class that met only once a week would be difficult and unrewarding if students were not prepared—specifically, if they didn't do the week's reading.

So David designed, and we've both since refined, the Structured Journal. For any assigned text, students track their thoughts in just four areas as they read:

- What confuses me, or what don't I understand completely?
- What are the most important parts or ideas in this section?
- How does this connect to what I'm learning from other texts and/or in class?
- What reflections or "I wonders" do I have?

We've used structured journaling as a way for students—from first graders to masters candidates—to read closely on their own and for us to hold

Toward a Gradual Release

Close reading is based on questions, and we're huge fans of questions. Questions are potent, offering support for students as they read, and directing attention to the section of text they need to pay attention to in order to respond. When well-written, questions can help students frame those responses and how they consider that portion of the text. We argue for lots of questions that point students to the places in the text where they're most likely to get stuck so they can wrestle with the textbase in those challenging parts. Pondering good questions and explaining answers, we've argued, is the chief way to deepen students' comprehension *and* develop a strong Standard of Coherence.

But our students don't always have us and our good questions with them. We need to help them move from answering our questions to taking responsibility for finding their own essential understanding, so they can independently read and comprehend deeply whenever they need and want to.

them accountable for doing so. It's powerful. At first, students will need you to "chunk" the text into manageable sections before they begin to journal. Eventually, they'll get the sense of how much text to read before they stop to journal. There's no singular answer, so help your students with this decision-making as long as they seem to need you to.

Essentially, structured journaling is an attempt to force readers to activate the cognitive processes most essential for reading. Invariably, reading well (understanding what you read) means reading more carefully and slowly. Therefore, many people find doing structured journaling extremely challenging, even when they can see it makes them far better readers. The goal of structured journaling is to make these practices into reading habits.

How to Teach Structured Journaling

While you can react and comment on any aspect of the text, tracking these four constructs as you're reading is a powerful way to connect to the text, prepare for discussion, and bring clarity to your reading. The order you track them in isn't important.

1. Ask yourself, "What don't I completely understand?" These might be references, words, or ideas that you just can't ponder your way to an understanding of. Make sure you note where you encountered them in the text.

2. Ask yourself, "What do I think are the most important ideas and/or parts, and why?"

3. Make connections to other relevant readings, classwork, learnings, or experiences.

4. Ask yourself, "What 'I wonder' questions or other responses do I have?" This is pushing beyond the text in some ways. It can be anything from wondering why authors are making the decisions they make to some related thought that something in the reading gave you. This is where the reading mind becomes invested in the major ideas and implications of what it has read.

Here are some observations that trended pretty consistently with regular use of structured journaling:

- Students initially have the most trouble determining what is important, which makes sense considering that requires more thought than determining the main idea. And there are no teacher- or publisher-created questions to point the way.

- Proficient readers can recognize what they don't understand or what confuses them better than weaker readers. This puzzled us until we realized that so much escapes weaker readers when they read, the thought of recording it all can be paralyzing. Proficient readers have less confusion, so recording it feels more manageable. So, you may need to adapt these questions or suggestions for weaker readers until they have the hang of it: "What four things confuse me?"; "What are two things I don't understand completely?"; and "List no more than one thing per paragraph."

- Most students find making connections the easiest and, in many ways, the most helpful skill to track.

- You'll likely need to provide examples of "I wonder" responses at first because few students are used to thinking beyond the confines of the page. After a while, we bet those responses will be a favorite source of discussion topics. After they get used to tracking their insights in this new way, all students, we've found, come up with insightful wonderings.

Many teachers have experienced the power of the structured journal. They found it especially helpful in generating discussions based on the reading their students were doing. They also found it works for informational as well as narrative texts. We've found that, too. The other thing teachers value about structured journaling is that they can carry on a conversation with even the most introverted students by responding to their entries, either by writing directly to them or by collecting and using entries to prepare for class discussion. College teachers interested in helping their students read and retain the course material have been especially taken with it, once they get over how hard it is for their college students those first few weeks.

Structured journaling is challenging. The cognitive load and the responsibility of figuring out what's most valuable to record and take away from reading a text shift completely to students. You'll see just how much scaffolding well-crafted, text-focused questions provide students when you try structured journaling. They will likely struggle at first without the support those questions offer.

Examples of Student Wonderings

- While reading *The Tale of Despereaux,* a second grader wondered why the author, Kate DiCamillo, seemed to emphasize how dark everything was at certain parts of the text, but how light it was at others. This led to a lively whole-class discussion of light symbolism in the book.

- A fifth grader, after reading an excerpt from *Insect* by Laurence Mound, that explained the importance of insects to the environment, wondered if there were no insects on Earth, would something else have replaced them and their functions.

- A fourth grader, reflecting on the nature of change while reading about states of matter, wondered if there's anything in the world that doesn't change.

- Following a read-aloud of Marcus Pfister's *The Rainbow Fish*, a first grader wondered how we can know when it's right to be proud and when it's wrong.

Text Annotation

Another great way to shift the cognitive load over to students is to teach them to annotate text, or mark it up, as they read it. That way, they can go back and quickly see what struck them.

How to Teach Text Annotation

There are about a zillion systems for annotating, and you may well already have your own. Following the ease-of-access and ease-of-implementation rule, here is one system we've taught with good results as early as third grade:

1. Tell students that, instead of answering questions, they're having a "conversation" with the text by marking it up and recording what they notice.

2. Put a question mark (**?**) next to any words, phrases, or concepts they don't understand. They can also circle or underline those words.

3. Put a checkmark (✔) next to anything they agree with.

4. Put an arrow (➜) next to anything they think is important.

5. Put an exclamation mark (**!**) in the margin next to anything that makes them wonder, and then say what they wonder in a few words next to it.

If this system seems to capture much of what the structured journal did, that is no coincidence! Both systems activate the most important cognitive activities students need to ensure comprehension. Marking what they notice is the hallmark of alert, engaged readers.

Here's what you must do with these more autonomous systems: *actively* teach your students how to do structured journaling and text annotation by doing lots of modeling and providing lots of feedback. We've all seen students' early attempts, which usually turn books into rainbows of highlighted text! It takes time, coaching, and practice for them to learn to track essential elements.

Similarly, as with all these different types of writing approaches, teachers have reported that doing the structured journal or annotating themselves is super helpful. Students have been responding to questions someone else wrote for them for years. These approaches put the responsibility to figure out much of what a text offers squarely in students' hands. Being unyoked from supportive questions and asked to analyze a text all on your own is a major step up in demand. That's not to say there's no role for questions. (Have we mentioned we're big fans of questions?)

Your systems for building understanding through writing must work equally well for you and your students. We're partial to the simplest of systems but encourage you to let your students experiment and adopt what works best for them, after you've taught them some different techniques.

Writing at the Sentence Level

We're making a shift here to more micro-writing—and to the idea of using writing at the sentence level to understand and better unpack complex syntax.

This is one of those important comprehension support keys—giving your students deeper understanding of the work different parts of the sentence do. This will draw on the important work connectives do to convey meaning that we looked at back in Chapter 5. Remember, connectives provide helpful clues to the relationships between propositions (idea units) in text. We can't assume young readers know the function of connectives and other signaling words and phrases, or what a given connective signifies. They're only helpful if students know what a given connective is signaling and are on the lookout for these sorts of cues. Cultivating this level of alertness is especially helpful for multilingual learners.

Meredith folded explicit teaching of connectives into her writing instruction starting with second graders on up. The list is organized loosely into what function the words served.

The list is also available as a printable resource. As you can see, it's organized from simpler to more elaborate versions of words in each category. Meredith has shared it with students from second grade through community college.

She modified this deceptively simple list from a thin, no-nonsense, spiral-bound book called *Teaching Basic Writing Skills*. No nonsense, indeed! It happened to be a terrific resource and became her go-to for remaking her own approach to teaching writing. It's out of print now but has been replaced by an expanded approach to writing, *The Writing Revolution*, by Dr. Judith C. Hochman and Natalie Wexler. As readers of *Know Better, Do Better* might remember, we sent our son to the Windward School, a learning disabilities school in White Plains, New York, where Dr. Hochman was then the head of school. We sent him there for his reading struggles, but he came out of it with many lessons for reading and writing instruction that we applied in our teaching at Family Academy and ever since.

Joining Words (Connectives)

Use this list to help you connect two ideas or parts of sentences. You can also use most of these words to move you to a new part of your paragraph, or from paragraph to paragraph.

All authors make use of these words. That means you can notice them when you read and understand what the author is signaling to you!

Time words (good for narrative or sequence writing):

as soon as	when	next
whenever	until	before
while	after a while	meanwhile
after	whenever	

Ways to make your point or move to the conclusion

since	yet	however
although	nevertheless	even if
even though	though	regardless
nonetheless	either...or	nonetheless

General Conjunctions

after	even if	nonetheless	till
although	even though	or	unless
and	for (because)	rather than	until
as	how	regardless of	when
as if	however	since	whenever
as though	if	so	where
as though	if...then	so that	wherever
because	in order that	than	while
before	in order to	that	yet
but	neither...nor	then	
either...or	nevertheless	though	

Change of direction words ("Adversatives")

but	however,	yet,
although,	nevertheless	on the other hand

Modified version of Judith Hochman's original, used by permission

Download a copy of "Joining Words" (Connectives).

The Value of Direct Instruction in Sentence-Level Writing

There are obvious implications for the power of directly teaching connectives to English learners and any students who may not have had much experience with these sorts of words, especially the more elaborate versions within each category. Students who know *but* may not know *to the contrary* or *however* and can be thrown off as a result.

In short, it's a good teaching tool that can help your students gain proficiency with connectives while becoming stronger, more "in control" writers. They'll also become more alert in the process.

We stand on the shoulders of giants and have been fortunate to apply and broadcast their genius through our own work. Two of those giants have worked at the sentence level of reading and writing better than anyone we know, except for maybe Mrs. Passatino, David's seventh-grade English teacher, who was the first person to see any talent in him, but also had him diagramming sentences all period long!

Lily Wong Fillmore and the Importance of "Juicy Sentence" Writing

Lily Wong Fillmore is a linguist who has done beautiful work demonstrating the value of having students investigate and construct "juicy sentences" (complex sentences packed with meaning) since she retired from Berkeley. Although she developed the work with and on behalf of young English learners, its power is universal. Many students for whom reading is hard work will shut down entirely when faced with a long, complex sentence. But longer, more complex sentences are a hallmark of rich, complex text. Being able to write a sentence and stay in control of the syntax is a sign of a skillful writer. That means students should work on juicy sentences regularly as they move up the grades. It's imperative we teach students they can navigate complex syntax, by providing the experiences that will enable them to do so.

We recommend a process designed to investigate juicy or complex sentences with your students, and it will become second nature once you get the hang of it. Rest assured, the sky's the limit on what students will discover. Regularly investigating how sentences convey meaning will make the textbase more accessible to all readers. It is definitely "work worth doing," which is why we recommended it in Chapter 7 as a component of close reading, during the third read. Then we look at a great method to help students produce their own juicy sentences.

Juicy sentences occur in every language!

Juicy Sentence Protocol

Pick a sentence from a text you're already working with. It should have complex syntax, yet be important or interesting to understand in light of the rest of the passage.

- Make sure to write it where everyone can see it at once (sentence strips are ideal; but chart paper or on a whiteboard is fine, too).
- Read it aloud (or ask a student volunteer to read it aloud) once or twice so every student has access to the sentence and its cadence.
- Check with students to see if there are any unknown vocabulary words.
- If so, teach them either with drop-in definitions (see Chapter 2, p. 50) or provide more thorough explanations for high-value words.
- Ask students to locate any internal punctuation to see how and why it sets clauses apart.
- Ask a volunteer to read the sentence aloud again so students can concentrate on how the punctuation affects the cadence of the sentence and sections it into chunks.

- Have students work together to find the subject and main verb (sentence kernel). At first, and as long as needed for primary students or English learners, this may stay teacher-supported.
- Once you have agreement, record the sentence kernel where students can see it.
- Ask what information each other part of the sentence provides. You can frame this as whether a chunk is providing information as to the "who, what, when, how, why" of the sentence kernel.
- For students who volunteer an answer, ask for clues they saw to support it. Check for understanding and consensus each time.
- As you discuss each chunk, add it back to the sentence kernel where it belongs until you finish exploring the sentence. This is where sentence strips are powerful. You can literally cut the juicy sentence into phrases or even cut it word by word to reconstruct and deconstruct the sentence.
- Finish by reading the sentence in the context of its paragraph in the text.

If you could do this protocol most days, say 3–4 times a week, the payoff in students' ability to navigate the textbase and parse challenging syntax would grow apace. Lily taught it as early as PreK, but it works in any grade.

Judith Hochman and the Importance of Sentence Expansion

In *The Writing Revolution*, Hochman introduces sentence writing with clear protocols and practice opportunities that can turn any student who has basic decoding into a successful writer of sentences. Her process of sentence expansion is essentially a writing-first inversion of the juicy sentence protocol described earlier.

Sentence expansion invites students to start with a sentence kernel and then to expand it into a more elaborate sentence. Hochman is also a proponent of writing about what you've read and using writing to help students solidify new knowledge. She offers models of sentence-kernel expansion that are applicable to any subject. Here's an example based on an elementary social studies topic so you can see how it works:

Content of Sentence	Function of the Part	Notes
Pyramids were built	Sentence kernel	Note the presence of a subject and verb making this a sentence.
When:	Each answer adds specific information which can be folded into the expanded sentence in a series of subordinate clauses.	in ancient times
Where:		in Egypt
Why:		to protect the body of the deceased pharaoh
Expanded Sentence: (Note the folding in of prepositions and the consideration of where clauses worked best for writing flow. This is manageable because the task is so clear and finite.)	Complete, complex sentence	In ancient times, pyramids were built in Egypt to protect the body of the deceased pharaoh.

(*The Writing Revolution*, pp. 59–60)

In addition to the symbiotic relationship of Fillmore and Hochman's processes, and that they both make the use of connectives to help readers bridge ideas in writing so clear and functional, there's another reason they're powerful. They both reinforce the idea that written language is designed to convey meaning. In this case, they go beyond grammar and syntax to express the idea that propositions—those idea units—exist in networks to do just that.

Helping students learn to read and write complex sentences is fun. It is also a potent way to show students how multiple propositions can be stacked up in a single sentence, causing that sentence to communicate a lot of ideas between its initial capital letter and its end punctuation. Putting students in the driver's seat and affording them the capacity to build and take apart such sentences is empowering. It will fuel their reading and propel their writing ability in ways that will please them and amaze you.

In Closing, Remember...

- Reading and writing have a reciprocal and supportive relationship.
- Writing about topics being studied can solidify and deepen learning about the topics.
- Brief writing and note-taking opportunities support close reading by bringing students back to the text, either to confirm their original response or clarify before writing.
- Writing in response to more complex text-dependent questions helps students organize their thinking. It does not have to be done with every question.
- Structured journaling and annotating text help shift responsibility for comprehension to the student.
- Being asked to explain their thinking while reading complex text helps students develop a strong Standard of Coherence.
- Unpacking and understanding complex sentences supports reading, writing, and thinking.
- Working with students to create more complex sentences is a potent way to show how multiple propositions can be stacked up in a single sentence.

The journey that brought us to the approaches and understandings we've shared with you in these pages so far was long and at times difficult. Along the way it was filled with mistakes, most of which we gained important learning from.

In our conclusion, we trace some of those mistakes and what we learned from them. We also lay claim to the most important aspects of literacy instruction we got right—eventually. We hope by ending *Know Better, Do Better: Comprehension* this way, we can save you from some of the missteps we've made over decades in the field.

Conclusion

The Family Academy's success in teaching almost all of our students to read well drew lots of attention, likely due to the fact we'd started at the absolute bottom (literally) in terms of outcomes. As a result, quite a few "distinguished visitors" (congress members, city councilors, NYC school chancellors, many authors, one mayor) requested visits to see what we were doing right, and we were happy to host them. Often when they left, they would say something to the effect that we had "overwhelmed the problem" by making reading, writing, speaking, and listening central to nearly every aspect of our students' day.

How We "Overwhelmed the Reading Problem"

Those visitors were right. We did "overwhelm our reading problem" by making all the instructional moves described in this book.

- We celebrated words in the school's hallways, common rooms, and classrooms (Chapter 2).
- We built knowledge, debated it, and made it a currency (Chapter 1).
- Every student, every day, read, talked about, and wrote about texts connected to science, history, and social studies as part of the General Knowledge Curriculum (Chapter 1).

- Teachers, students, and school leaders were invited to be curious and act on their curiosity.

- All students read grade-level text and engaged in "textual analysis" (close reading) four days a week, and explained their thinking multiple times a day in writing and lively discussions (Chapter 7).

- All students participated in literature groups, where they read, discussed, and wrote about full-length works of fiction, four hours a week (Chapter 6).

- All students went to the library once a week to pick out books to read on their own—books often connected to topics they were studying.

- We valued discourse and giving voice to every student.

- We spent our faculty meetings refining the curriculum, and our teaching and learning evolved based on new research David had unearthed.

- We celebrated students' accomplishments in reading and writing with families (and always served lots of good food!).

Our Guiding Principles

We hope you've seen our guiding principles embedded throughout the book. Here, we recap them for you:

- 🌐 Build listening and speaking into any sequence of text-based activities, along with reading and writing. If rich, interactive student-dominated discussions aren't part of your close-reading work with texts, it's unlikely your students' comprehension will catch fire. If there isn't a ton of social learning and collective building of insights, too many students will be left behind. That work can be in small groups, pairs of students interacting, linguistic partnerships to support students just learning English ... what is essential is getting your students talking about the reading they are doing together.

- 🌐 Provide for the differing needs of students, considering the needs of English learners in particular. That means providing and scaffolding supports differently. It doesn't mean asking some students easier questions or substituting a simpler, less rich text for some readers. We've all (or almost all) done that and it doesn't work.

- Encourage your students to hang in there (and support one another) when questions are challenging or the text is proving difficult. This mantra might help: "Reread it. Think about it again. Try to explain to yourself why you are confused. Talk about it. Write about it."

- Make room for students questioning the text beyond or instead of the questions you generated. Celebrate that spirit of inquiry and curiosity and find ways to build discussions or extension activities around students' questions. They won't always have you in their lives, but they can have the mental habit of questioning text for keeps, if you inculcate it!

- Make sure students explain their thinking and what evidence they used in arriving at their answers. This makes their thinking visible to themselves to the rest of the class and to us.

Watch David and Meredith discuss the potency of self-explanation as a centerpiece of improving comprehension.

In the introduction, we cataloged a litany of mistakes we made at our own school. We made many and, thankfully, learned from them. But we also got a lot of things right which are worth noting.

Above all, what we got right was creating a rich schoolwide culture of literacy. We developed and implemented many of the approaches described in this book and in *Know Better, Do Better: Teaching the Foundations So Every Child Can Read*. Those approaches grew out of reading and thinking about the cognitive science that undergirds all of reading. We communicated

with, learned from, and trusted our students. The same was true for parents and teachers, and we considered them our partners. By explaining science-based classroom practice to them, we became skilled at explaining it to other stakeholders. Among them were the career and technical (CTE) students and staff Meredith taught in Vermont, and the rural, urban, and suburban teachers David worked with as a consultant. We worked together to teach new CTE teachers fresh from their trades how to work effectively with students who lacked solid reading and writing skills. Doing this work in a setting far removed from the Family Academy in Harlem, extended our awareness of how widespread problems in reading instruction were.

Nonetheless, We Found New Ways to Make Unintentional Errors

Despite our range of experiences and knowledge, when we joined the national conversation in support of the Common Core State Standards for reading, we found new ways to make unintentional errors. Many of them came while we were leading the ELA work at Student Achievement Partners, founded to support implementation efforts after the standards were so widely adopted. In the spirit of knowing better, we want to fess up to some of them. It's the right thing to do, and many may resonate with you.

We knew well the importance of foundational skills. Yet, at this key moment, we didn't emphasize them. Instead, we focused our considerable energy and resources on what was new and radical about the CCSS, which were:

- access to rich and complex text for all students.
- the importance of being able to locate and discuss textual evidence.
- the role of knowledge building in reading success.

The fact was, the CCSS for foundational skills weren't anything new. But they were (and are) excellent because they were written by Louisa Moats and Marilyn Adams, revered reading researchers who'd been working in this area for years.

But what gets talked about gets attention. At a crucial point when we should have called out the fundamental role of foundational reading in building sturdy, self-reliant readers, we didn't. When we realized that mistake, we did our best to address it. Know better and move on.

In our advisory work with publishers, in presentations to educators, and in our staff development work with districts and schools, we hadn't strongly enough considered teacher creativity and the importance of working to earn teachers' trust. That, despite our collective 50 years teaching in classrooms!

Yet, we believe teachers should have a voice in any changes an administrator is considering making, particularly changes related to practice based in the science of reading. The success of those changes rests, after all, on teachers.

We (along with many others) are asking teachers to make a lot of big changes in how they teach children to read. Keeping teachers central to the conversation is more important than ever. Reading confidently and well is a joyous ingredient in a child's life. Teachers are the adults in our schools who can inculcate this joy most directly. Teachers need the knowledge of what it takes to create strong readers and then they need to be supported in developing the conditions to do so.

For change to happen, we all need to acknowledge what we've done well in the past and what we could've done better, as we've pretty much been doing since the start of this chapter. We agree with our friend Kareem Weaver that we need more humbleness in this work, *especially* from people like us who advise others about the vital work of teaching reading.

It's wrong to ask teachers to take on this hard work if other educators and those, like us, who advise in education are unwilling to do it. Changing how you approach a major aspect of your teaching is difficult. For our part, we deeply honor teachers for their willingness to engage in this hard work.

Lessons We Learned While Writing This Book

Everything about writing a book is hard, although you do learn a lot. But one of the hardest things about writing this book was conveying the idea that features of text that we adult readers process easily (so easily, in fact, we're often unaware that it's happening) can trip up less experienced readers and students learning English. Review Chapter 5 for details and examples of these features and others. We had to slow down our reading and scour lots of elementary school texts to find those examples. Fortunately, the features that trip up students most frequently are fairly easy to spot, such as:

- pronouns that are hard to trace back to their antecedent noun.
- propositions (units of meaning) that can only be comprehended if connected to earlier parts of the text.
- relative clauses that can make it hard to parse a sentence's meaning.
- proposition density within sentences or throughout a text.

It's important to raise students' awareness of those features whenever they reveal themselves. And that's best done by frequently addressing questions related to those features and having students explain their thinking through vibrant class discussions.

The essential roles of vocabulary and knowledge to achieve reading comprehension—or to thwart it—were reconfirmed in researching for this book. We're glad we gave them each their own full chapter. We're also glad that knowledge is getting its moment in the reading spotlight these days and we hope that doesn't change. We want vocabulary to share the spotlight. After all, reading has a lot to do with words!

The best way to grow knowledge and vocabulary is by reading a lot—in other words, by increasing reading volume. However, reading volume is one of the most neglected and challenging aspects of ELA instruction. Increasing reading volume is not always easy, especially when students aren't that crazy about reading—yet! But it's super important to keep trying for the types of simple solutions we presented in Chapter 1.

We realized something else: An emphasis on reading volume was something balanced literacy got right (especially for students who learned to read easily, requiring minimal explicit instruction). We've seen the value of students reading daily for periods of sustained time. What balanced literacy got terribly wrong about independent reading was labeling children as having a single reading level and failing to understand that not all reading volume is created equal. A volume of reading that's based on a topic and stays on it for some time, via a series of texts or a robust full-length text, grows more knowledge, along with more Tier 2 vocabulary. Both are crucial to students who need our support.

In Closing, Remember...

- "Overwhelming the reading problem" through a culture that celebrates reading, writing, speaking, listening, and language is doable and enormously valuable. We did it, and you can, too.

- Reading is an integrated process. Isolating any one element is a formula for disaster.

- You have to read the text carefully before you teach it. Learning how to read with an eye to what features of text might trip up your students is vital.

- If we want strong readers, it's crucial they engage in a large volume of reading.

- Strong readers are joyous readers.

- Teacher creativity and autonomy are crucial ingredients in improving reading comprehension. Teachers always need to be in the conversation about how to strengthen instruction and outcomes.

- We've made our share of mistakes. We've tried to learn from them so we can "know better and do better" and share those lessons with you.

In too many ways, our ELA instruction has been backwards. For decades, we didn't teach foundational skills systematically. We failed to embrace a systematic approach to phonics that is essential to learning how written English works. Lately, many schools and districts have been working to change that, and many of them are getting positive results. More students are reading with automatic word recognition and fluency. Hurray for that!

But many schools and districts that shunned teaching phonics systematically were, ironically, taking a rigidly systematic approach to comprehension by teaching students a series of discrete elements such as strategies and standards. We hope we've helped you understand the true nature of reading comprehension. We also hope we've shown you some useful instructional approaches that not only align with the science, but also build in space for the joy and intellectual satisfaction that making meaning from books and other rich texts brings to kids.

It's our hope and intent to be useful to those who, day in and day out, support students' learning. Writing is hard but teaching is harder. We wish you well, and hope you remain curious and steadfast in your work, and now that you know better, you keep doing better!

Resources

Part I: What Kids Need to Know to Comprehend Texts

Knowledge

Book Basket Challenge: This has been enormously helpful for teachers and schools that are making the shift from leveled reading/balanced reading approach toward a more research-validated approach to reading. To find out more about how to reorganize your leveled reading library into topical baskets, search for the Book Basket Project on the Achieve the Core website.

Companion Text Sets for the Read-Aloud Project (Grades PreK–2): To find many high-quality read-aloud books on diverse topics, search for ELA/Literacy Lessons on the Achieve the Core website. You can apply filters to narrow your search.

Text Set Project (Grades 2–12): You can also search the ELA/Literacy Lessons on the Achieve the Core website to find text sets created by teams of teachers and curated by seasoned reviewers under the auspices of Student Achievement Partners. There are hundreds of text sets searchable by grade level or date added or cultural relevance.

Mirrors, Windows, and Sliding Glass Doors: You can find a lovely, short video from Reading Rockets, where Rudine Sims Bishop discusses the origins of her thinking about children's literature as mirrors, windows, and sliding glass doors.

Scholastic Classroom Magazines: Get fresh, high-interest, knowledge-building content delivered all year long—in print, online, or both. Every single story, video, and activity is designed to hook your students and keep them engaged.

Vocabulary

The Academic Word Finder on the Achieve the Core site was developed by cognitive scientists and is a powerful free tool to help you select high-value words from any text passage. Simply upload a text and select what grade it is intended for and it will return results of which academic words are grade level, and which are going to be encountered later in a student's career. You can sign up to store your results or you can just use the Academic Word Finder without registering.

Teaching Phonics & Word Study in the Intermediate Grades, 3rd Edition, **by Wiley Blevins.** We're big fans of Wiley Blevins for anything to do with foundational reading. He, like us, emphasizes the importance of providing students with adequate repetition through practice opportunities so they can cement their learning. The reason we're recommending this book is because it's terrific, but also because he has wonderful, easy-to-implement morphology exercises that provide exposure to high-value Latin and Greek roots, along with high-frequency affixes.

Burnaby Welcome Center: This English learner resource site is maintained for free by the Burnaby Welcome Center in Burnaby, British Columbia (Canada). It's a treasure trove. A particular gold mine is their list of recommended academic vocabulary to teach annually Grades K–12. It is available in a half dozen languages to assist with parent communication.

The **List of Conjunctions** on this book's companion website was adapted by Meredith from Judith Hochman's *Teaching Basic Writing Skills*.

Vocabulary Resources are on the Reading Rockets website, which is maintained by its sponsor, WETA, Washington, D.C.'s public television provider. There are wonderful articles and practical tools and tips for teachers and parents alike.

The Significance of Vocabulary in the Common Core State Standards is a good synthesis David wrote to clarify the crucial role vocabulary study plays in students' ability to read grade-level complex text. It has practice exercises for selecting which words to teach from a variety of texts at different grade levels and then offers commentary on the model selections we made after teachers have a chance to work through their own thinking.

TextProject is the site where Elfrieda H. (Freddy) Hiebert maintains wonderful free resources. She was first and foremost a vocabulary maven, so we are listing the TextProject here. Truly, the resources she offers, along with her entire corpus of research, are resources that will overlap with every chapter in our book.

Word Nerds: Teaching All Students to Learn and Love Vocabulary **by Brenda J. Overturf, Leslie H. Montgomery, and Margot Holmes Smith** (Routledge). This book is written by three longtime teachers from Louisville and is a complete package of teacher- and student-friendly research-based practices and tips. They also pay careful attention to creating a culture where word discoveries are celebrated.

Morphology and Etymology

Learn That Word has a massive list of roots and affixes. Learnthat.org is a not-for-profit organization.

The Root Words and Affixes list on the Reading Rockets website will provide much of what you'd need—at least at first.

Teaching Morphology to Improve Literacy: A Guide for Teachers **by Nikki Zeh.** Zeh wrote this practical guide as part of her master's degree work at the University of Western Ontario. Its practicality, simplicity, and usefulness are clear from the number of places that also cite it as a good resource!

Big Words for Young Readers: Teaching Kids in Grades K to 5 to Decode—and Understand—Words With Multiple Syllables and Morphemes **by Heidi Anne Mesmer.** Mesmer shares essential background on how language "works," provides a K–5 scope and sequence to guide practice, and offers abundant research-backed strategies that you can put into action immediately.

Part II: What You Need to Know to Fuel the Reading Brain

Creating Text-Dependent Questions: Search for ELA/Literacy Text-Dependent Questions on the Achieve the Core website for resources we developed about how to write strong text-dependent questions that get at the places in the text that are crucial for students' understanding and reading growth. There are also tools for evaluating the quality of ready-made questions. Meredith's favorite tool here takes the qualitative analysis of the text selection you're planning to focus on with students and converts it straight into the questions that grow out of the richest, most complex aspects of any assigned reading.

Placing Text at the Center of the Standards-Aligned ELA Classroom from Meredith Liben and Susan Pimental can also be found on the Achieve the Core website. It lays out the reasons why text and students should be centered in every ELA classroom. In many ways, this brief is a compressed version of this whole book.

Part III: What You Can Do to Fuel the Reading Brain

Close-Reading Model Lessons on the Achieve the Core website are examples of close reading that follow along the lines we laid out as important, including proving your answer by providing textual evidence. Many of the examples in this book came from this collection.

Framework for Preparing, Implementing, and Assessing Close-Reading Lessons on the Achieve the Core website was developed by David. This framework is more elaborate than the simple system we showed you here, but it aligns with it. The framework links through to many of the key resources we developed during our time with Student Achievement Resources that reinforce or extend some of the understandings we've laid out here. It is a useful resource.

Text Complexity Resources can be found on the Achieve the Core website. You can go as deep as you want through that network of links, or you can just get the basics of text complexity. There is lots of good information and many useful tools available to you there.

Robust Comprehension Instruction with Questioning the Author: 15 Years Smarter is the second book by Isabel L. Beck, Margaret G. McKeown, and Cheryl A. Sandora on their approach. It is chock-full of ideas, reflections from teachers, and ideas for embedding vocabulary instruction (what Beck and McKeown have been primarily known for) and writing into these text-centered lessons.

The Writing Revolution website and book of the same name contain many resources on teaching writing effectively using a content approach.

Writing for Understanding: Using Backward Design to Help All Students Write Effectively is put out by the Vermont Writing Collaborative. This is a great read and a terrific resource for writing. It's available on the collaborative's website or through Amazon.

References

Adams, M. J. (1991). Beginning to read: Thinking and learning about print. *Language, 67*, 388.

Adams, M. J. (2009). The challenge of advanced texts: The interdependence of reading and learning. In E. H. Hiebert (Ed.), *Reading more, reading better: Are American students reading enough of the right stuff?* (pp. 163–189). Guilford Press.

Baker, E. A., & McKeown, M. (2009, September 7). *Comprehension instruction: Focus on content or strategies* [Audio podcast]. Voice of Literacy. https://sites.libsyn.com/469683/vol/comprehension-instruction-focus-on-content-or-strategies-with-dr-margaret-mckeown

Beck, I. L., McKeown, M. G., & Kucan, L. (2003). Taking delight in words: Using oral language to build young children's vocabularies. *American Educator, 27*, 36–46.

Beck, I. L., McKeown, M. G., & Kucan, L. (2008). *Creating robust vocabulary: Frequently asked questions & extended examples.* Guilford Press.

Beck, I. L., McKeown, M. G., & Kucan, L. (2013). *Bringing words to life: Robust vocabulary instruction* (second edition). Guilford Press.

Beck, I. L., McKeown, M. G., Sandora, C., Kucan, L., & Worthy, J. (1996). Questioning the author: A yearlong classroom implementation to engage students with text. *The Elementary School Journal, 96*(4), 385–414.

Best, R., Ozuru, Y., Floyd, R., & McNamara, D. S. (2006). Children's text comprehension: Effects of genre, knowledge, and text cohesion. In S. A. Barab, K. E. Hay, D. T. Hickey (Eds.), *Proceedings of the Seventh International Conference of the Learning Sciences* (pp. 37–42). Erlbaum.

Biemiller, A. (2010). *Words worth teaching: Closing the vocabulary gap.* SRA/McGraw-Hill.

Binder, K. S., Cote, N. G., Lee, C., Bessette, E., & Vu, H. (2017). Beyond breadth: The contributions of vocabulary depth to reading comprehension among skilled readers. *Journal of Research in Reading, 40*(3), 333–343.

Bishop, R. (1990). Mirrors, windows and sliding glass doors. *Perspectives: Choosing and Using Books for the Classroom, 6*(3), ix–xi.

Bisra, K., Liu, Q., Nesbit, J. C., Salimi, F., & Winne, P. H. (2018). Inducing self-explanation: A meta-analysis. *Educational Psychology Review, 30*(3), 703–725.

Bowers, P. N., & Kirby, J. R. (2010). Effects of morphological instruction on vocabulary acquisition. *Reading and Writing, 23*(5), 515–537.

Brown, L. T., Mohr, K. A. J., Bradley, R. W., & Barrett, T. S. (2017). The effects of dyad reading and text difficulty on third-graders' reading development. *The Journal of Educational Research, 111*(5), 541–553.

Burns, M. K., Duke, N. K., & Cartwright, K. B. (2023). Evaluating components of the active view of reading as intervention targets: Implications for social justice. *School Psychology, 38*(1), 30–41.

Cabell, S. (2020). Building content knowledge to boost comprehension in the primary grades. *Reading Research Quarterly, 55*, 99–107.

Cain, K., & Oakhill, J. V. (1999). Inference making ability and its relation to comprehension failure in young children. *Reading & Writing, 11*, 489–503.

Cain, K., & Oakhill, J. V. (2006). Profiles of children with specific reading comprehension difficulties. *British Journal of Educational Psychology, 76*(4), 683–69.

Cain, K., & Oakhill, J. V. (2014). Reading comprehension and vocabulary: Is vocabulary more important for some aspects of comprehension? *L'Année Psychologique, 114*, 647–662.

Cain, K., Oakhill, J. V., Barnes, M. A., & Bryant, P. E. (2001). Comprehension skill, inference-making ability, and their relation to knowledge. *Memory & Cognition, 29*(6), 850–859.

Cervantes, A. (2019). *Lety out loud.* Scholastic.

Cervetti, G. N., Wright, T. S., & Hwang, H. (2016). Conceptual coherence, comprehension, and vocabulary acquisition: A knowledge effect? *Reading and Writing, 29*(4), 761–779.

Cervetti, G. N., & Wright , T. S. (2020). The role of knowledge in understanding and learning from text. In E. B. Moje, P. P. Afflerbach, P. Enciso, N. K. Lesaux (Eds.), *Handbook of reading research* (Volume 5). Routledge.

Chall, J. S., & Jacobs, V. A. (2003). Poor children's fourth-grade slump. *American Educator*, Spring 2003.

Chi, M. T. H., Bassok, M., Lewis, M. W., Reimann, P., & Glaser, R. (1989). Self-explanations: How students study and use examples in learning to solve problems. *Cognitive Science, 13*, 145–182.

Chi, M. T. H., de Leeuw, N., Chiu, M., & LaVancher, C. (1994). Eliciting self-explanations improves understanding. *Cognitive Science, 18*, 439–477.

Cho, Y. H., & Jonassen, D. H. (2012). Learning by self-explaining causal diagrams in high-school biology. *Asia Pacific Education Review, 13*(1), 171–184.

Chomsky, C. (2002). When you still can't read in third grade: After decoding, what? In S. J. Samuels (Ed.), *What research has to say about reading Instruction* (pp. 13–30). International Reading Association.

Cognitive psychology and cognitive neuroscience/Situation models and inferencing. (2020, January 19). Wikibooks.

Cunningham, A. E., & Stanovich, K. E. (1998). What reading does for the mind. *American Educator, 22*, 8–17.

Currie, N. K., & Cain, K. (2015). Children's inference generation: The role of vocabulary and working memory. *Journal of Experimental Child Psychology, 137*, 57–75.

Dijk, T. A., & Kintsch, W. (1983). *Strategies of discourse comprehension*. Academic Press.

Dohower, S. L. (1987). Effects of repeated reading on second-grade transitional readers' fluency and comprehension. *Reading Research Quarterly, 22*(4), 389–406.

Ehri, L. C. (2014). Orthographic mapping in the acquisition of sight word reading, spelling memory, and vocabulary learning. *Scientific Studies of Reading, 18*(1), 5–21.

Ehri, L. C. (2023). Phases of development in learning to read and spell words. *American Educator, 47*(3), 17–18.

Elbro, C., & Buch-Iversen, I. (2013). Activation of background knowledge for inference making: Effects on reading comprehension. *Scientific Studies of Reading, 17*, 435–452.

Elleman, A. M., Lindo, E. J., Morphy, P., & Compton, D. L. (2009). The impact of vocabulary instruction on passage-level comprehension of school-age children: A meta-analysis. *Journal of Research on Educational Effectiveness, 2*(1), 1–44.

Ericsson, K. A., & Kintsch, W. (1995). Long-term working memory. *Psychological Review, 102*(2), 211–245.

Ferreira, F., Bailey, K. G. D., & Ferraro, V. (2002). Good-enough representations in language comprehension. *Current Directions in Psychological Science, 11*(1), 11–15.

Fordham, N. W., Wellman, D., & Sandmann, A. (2002). Taming the text: Engaging and supporting students in social studies readings. *The Social Studies, 93*(4), 149–158.

Garner, R., & Gillingham, M. G. (1991). Topic knowledge, cognitive interest, and text recall: A microanalysis. *Journal of Experimental Education, 59*(4), 310–319.

Givón, T. (1995). Coherence in the text and coherence in the mind. In M. A. Gernsbacher & T. Givón (Eds.), *Coherence in spontaneous text* (pp. 59–115). Benjamins.

Graesser, A. C., McNamara, D. S., & Louwerse, M. M. (2003). What readers need to learn in order to process coherence relations in narrative and expository text. In A. P. Sweet & C. E. Snow (Eds.), *Rethinking reading comprehension* (pp. 82–98). Guilford Press.

Graesser, A. C., Singer, M., & Trabasso, T. (1994). Constructing inferences during narrative text comprehension. *Psychological Review, 101*(3), 371–395.

Graham, S. & Hebert, M. A. (2010). *Writing to read: Evidence for how writing can improve reading*. A Carnegie Corporation Time to Act Report. Alliance for Excellent Education.

Guthrie, J. T., McRae, A., Coddington, C. S., Lutz, K. S., Wigfield, A., & Barbosa, P. (2009). Impacts of comprehensive reading instruction on diverse outcomes of low- and high-achieving readers. *Journal of Learning Disabilities, 42*(3), 195–214.

Hadley, E. B., Dickinson, D. K., Hirsh-Pasek, K., & Golinkoff, R. M. (2019). Building semantic networks: The impact of a vocabulary intervention on preschoolers' depth of word knowledge. *Reading Research Quarterly, 54*(1), 41–61.

Hatkoff, I., Hatkoff, C., & Kahumbu, P. (2006). *Owen & Mzee: The true story of a remarkable friendship*. Scholastic.

Hawkins, J., Ginty, E., Kurzman, K. L., Leddy, D., & Miller, J. (2008). *Writing for understanding: Using backward design to help all students write effectively*. Vermont Writing Collaborative.

Hiebert, E. H. (2009). The (mis)match between texts and students who depend on schools to become literate. In E. H. Hiebert & M. Sailors (Eds.), *Finding the right texts: What works for beginning and struggling readers* (pp. 1–20). Guilford Press.

Hiebert, E. H., & Bravo, M. (2010). Morphological knowledge and learning to read. In D. Wyse, R. Andrews, & J. Hoffman (Eds.), *The Routledge International Handbook of English, Language and Literacy Teaching* (pp. 87–97). Routledge.

Hiebert, E. H., Goodwin, A. P., & Cervetti, G. N. (2018). Core vocabulary: Its morphological content and presence in exemplar texts. *Reading Research Quarterly, 53*(1), 29–49.

Hochman, J. C., & Wexler, N. (2017). *The writing revolution: A guide to advancing thinking through writing in all subjects and grades*. Jossey-Bass.

Hwang, H., Cabell, S. Q., & Joyner, R. E. (2022). Effects of integrated literacy and content-area instruction on vocabulary and comprehension in the elementary years: A meta-analysis. *Scientific Studies of Reading, 26*(3), 223–249.

Kendeou, P., McMaster, K. L., & Christ, T. J. (2016). Reading comprehension: Core components and processes. *Policy Insights from the Behavioral and Brain Sciences, 3*(1), 62–69.

Kintsch, W. (1998). *Comprehension: A paradigm for cognition*. Cambridge University Press.

Kintsch, W. (2005). An overview of top-down and bottom-up effects in comprehension: The CI perspective. *Discourse Processes, 39*, 125–128.

Kintsch, W. (2009). Learning and constructivism. In S. Tobias & T. M. Duffy (Eds.), *Constructivist instruction: Success or failure?* (pp. 223–241). Routledge/Taylor & Francis Group.

Kintsch, W. (2019). Revisiting the construction-integration model of text comprehension and its implications for instruction. In D. E. Alvermann, N. J. Unrau, & R. B. Ruddell (Eds.), *Theoretical models and processes of literacy* (7th ed., pp. 178–203). Routledge.

Kintsch W., & Kintsch, E. (2005). Comprehension. In S. G. Paris and S. A. Stahl (Eds.), *Children's reading comprehension and assessment* (pp. 71–92). Lawrence Erlbaum.

Kintsch, W., & van Dijk, T. A. (1978). Toward a model of text comprehension and production. *Psychological Review, 85*(5), 363–394.

Kirby, J. R., & Bowers, P. N. (2017). Morphological instruction and literacy: Binding phonological, orthographic, and semantic features of words. In K. Cain, D. L. Compton, and R. K. Parrila (Eds.), *Theories of reading development* (pp. 437–462). John Benjamins.

LaBerge, D., & Samuels, S. J. (1974). Toward a theory of automatic information processing in reading. *Cognitive Psychology, 6*(2), 293–323.

Landauer, T. K., & Dumais, S. T. (1997). A solution to Plato's problem: The latent semantic analysis theory of acquisition, induction, and representation of knowledge. *Psychological Review, 104*(2), 211.

Lee, J., & Yoon, S. Y. (2017). The effects of repeated reading on reading fluency for students with reading disabilities: A meta-analysis. *Journal of Learning Disabilities, 50*(2), 213–224.

Liben, M., & Pimentel, S. (2018). *Placing text at the center of the standards-aligned ELA classroom*. https://achievethecore.org/page/3185/placing-text-at-the-center-of-the-standards-aligned-ela-classroom

Lupo, S. M., Strong, J. Z., Lewis, W. E., & Walpole, S. (2018). Building background knowledge through reading: Rethinking text sets. *Journal of Adolescent & Adult Literacy, 61*(4) 433–444.

McKeown, M. G., Beck, I. L., & Blake, R. G. (2009). Reading comprehension instruction: Focus on content or strategies? *Perspectives on Language and Literacy, 35*(2), 28.

McKeown, M. G., Beck, I. L., & Blake, R. G. (2009). Rethinking reading comprehension instruction: A comparison of instruction for strategies and content approaches. *Reading Research Quarterly, 44*(3), 218–253.

McNamara, D. S. (2010). Strategies to read and learn: Overcoming learning by consumption. *Medical Education, 44*, 340–346.

McNamara, D. S. (2017). Self-explanation and reading strategy training (SERT) improves low-knowledge students' science course performance. *Discourse Processes, 54*(7), 479–492.

Murphy, J. (2001). *The great fire*. Scholastic.

Nagy, W., Anderson, R. C., Schommer, M., Scott, J. A., & Stallman, A. C. (1989). Morphological families in the internal lexicon. *Reading Research Quarterly, 24*(3), 262–282.

Narvaez, D., van den Broek, P., & Ruiz, A. B. (1999). The influence of reading purpose on inference generation and comprehension in reading. *Journal of Educational Psychology, 91*(3), 488–496.

National Governors Association Center for Best Practices & Council of Chief State School Officers. (2010). *Common Core State Standards for English language arts and literacy in history/social studies, science, and technical subjects*. Washington, D.C.

National Reading Panel. (2000). *Teaching children to read: An evidence-based assessment of the scientific research literature on reading and its implications for reading instruction*. National Institute of Child Health and Human Development.

Neuman, S. B., & Kaefer, T. (2018). Developing low-income children's vocabulary and content knowledge through a shared book reading program. *Contemporary Educational Psychology*, 15–24.

Neuman, S. B., Newman, E. H., & Dwyer, J. (2011). Educational effects of a vocabulary intervention on preschoolers' word knowledge and conceptual development: A cluster-randomized trial. *Reading Research Quarterly, 46*(3), 249–272.

Oudega, M., & van den Broek, P. (2018). Standards of coherence in reading: Variations in processing and comprehension of text. In K. K. Mills, D. Long, J. Magliano, and K. Wiemer (Eds.), *Deep comprehension* (pp. 41–51). Routledge.

Ouellette, G. P. (2006). What's meaning got to do with it? The role of vocabulary in word reading and reading comprehension. *Journal of Educational Psychology, 98*, 554–566.

Padak, N., Newton, E., Rasinski, T., & Newton, R. M. (2008). Getting to the root of word study: Teaching Latin and Greek word roots in elementary and middle grades. In A. E. Farstrup & S. J. Samuels (Eds.), *What research has to say about vocabulary instruction* (pp. 1–27). International Literacy Association.

Paige, D. D., Rasinski, T., Magpuri-Lavell, T., & Smith, G. S. (2014). Interpreting the relationships among prosody, automaticity, accuracy, and silent reading comprehension in secondary students. *Journal of Literacy Research, 46*(2), 123–156.

Pearson, D. P., & Liben, D. (2015). *The progression of reading comprehension*. Achieve the Core. https://achievethecore.org/page/1195/the-progression-of-reading-comprehension

Perfetti, C. (2007). Reading ability: Lexical quality to comprehension. *Scientific Studies of Reading, 11*(4), 357–383.

Perfetti, C., & Stafura, J. (2014). Word knowledge in a theory of reading comprehension. *Scientific Studies of Reading, 18*, 22–37.

Pressley, M., Wood, E., Woloshyn, V., Martin, V., King, A., & Menke, D. (1992). Encouraging mindful use of prior knowledge: Attempting to construct explanatory answers facilitates learning. *Educational Psychology, 27*, 91–109.

Raudszus, H., Segers, E., & Verhoeven, L. (2021). Patterns and predictors of reading comprehension growth in first and second language readers. *Journal of Research in Reading, 44*(2), 400–417.

Recht, D. R., & Leslie, L. (1988). Effect of prior knowledge on good and poor readers' memory of text. *Journal of Educational Psychology, 80*(1), 16–20.

Ryan, P. M. (2000). *Esperanza rising*. Scholastic.

Ryan, C. (1988). *Every living thing*. Turtleback Books.

Rylant, C. (1992). *Missing May*. Scholastic.

Samuels, S. J. (1979) The method of repeated readings. *The Reading Teacher, 32*, 403–408.

Schneider, W., Körkel, J., & Weinert, F. (1989). Domain-specific knowledge and memory performance: A comparison of high- and low-aptitude children. *Journal of Educational Psychology, 81*, 306–312.

Scientific Advisory Committee of the Knowledge Matters Campaign. (2023). *Four-part blogpost series in ASCD*. https://www.ascd.org/blogs/helping-students-access-complex-knowledge-rich-texts

Seidenberg, M. S., & Borkenhagen, M. C. (2020). Reading science and educational practice: Some tenets for teachers. *The Reading League Journal, 1*(1), 7–11.

Seidenberg, M. S., Borkenhagen, M. C., & Kearns, D. M. (2020). Lost in translation? Challenges in connecting reading science and educational practice. *Reading Research Quarterly, 55*, S19–S130.

Shanahan, T. (2016). Teaching reading comprehension and comprehension strategies. *Shanahan on Literacy*. https://www.shanahanonliteracy.com/blog/teaching-reading-comprehension-and-comprehension-strategies

Shanahan, T. (2018). What should morphology instruction look like? *Reading Rockets*. https://www.readingrockets.org/blogs/shanahan-on-literacy/what-should-morphology-instruction-look

Shanahan, T. (2023). What about the new research that says phonics isn't very important? *Shanahan on Literacy*. https://www.shanahanonliteracy.com/blog/what-about-the-new-research-that-says-phonics-instruction-isnt-very-important

Smith, R., Snow, P., Serry, T., & Hammond, L. (2021). The role of background knowledge in reading comprehension: A critical review. *Reading Psychology, 42*(3), 214–240.

Snow, C. (2010). Academic language and the challenge of reading for learning about science. *Science, 328*, 450–452.

Snow, E. L., Jacovina, M. E., Jackson, G. T., & McNamara, D. S. (2016). iSTART-2: A reading comprehension and strategy instruction tutor. In S. A. Crossley & D. S. McNamara (Eds.), *Adaptive educational technologies for literacy instruction* (pp. 104–121). Taylor & Francis.

Soto, C., de Blume, A. P. G., Jacovina, M., McNamara, D., Benson, N., Riffo, B., & Kruk, R. (2019). Reading comprehension and metacognition: The importance of inferential skills. *Cogent Education, 6*(1), Article: 1565067.

Stahl, S. A. (1991). Beyond the instrumentalist hypothesis: Some relationships between word meanings and comprehension. In P. Schwanenflugel (Ed.), *The psychology of word meanings* (pp. 157–178). Lawrence Erlbaum Associates.

Stahl, S., Chou Hare, V., Sinatra, R., & Gregory, J. (1991). Defining the role of prior knowledge and vocabulary in reading comprehension: The retiring of number 41. *Journal of Reading Behavior, 23*(4), 487–508.

Stanovich, K. E. (1986). Matthew effects in reading: Some consequences of individual differences in the acquisition of literacy. *Reading Research Quarterly, 21*(4), 360–407.

Van den Broek, P., & Helder, A. (2017). Cognitive processes in discourse comprehension: Passive processes, reader-initiated processes, and evolving mental representations. *Discourse Processes, 54*(5–6), 360–372.

Voss, J. F., & Silfies, L. N. (1996). Learning from history text: The interaction of knowledge and comprehension skill with text structure. *Cognition and Instruction, 14*(1), 45–68.

Wallace, R., Pearman, C., Hail, C., & Hurst, B. (2007). Writing for comprehension. *Reading Horizons: A Journal of Literacy and Language Arts, 48*(1).

Washington, J. A., & Seidenberg, M. S. (2021). Teaching reading to African American children: When home and school language differ. *American Educator*, Summer 2021, 26–40.

Whalley, K., & Hansen, J. (2006). The role of prosodic sensitivity in children's reading development. *Journal of Research in Reading, 29*, 288–303.

Whipple, G. M. (1925). Report of the National Committee on Reading (Twenty-fourth Yearbook of the National Society for the Study of Education, Part I). Bloomington, IL: Public School Publishing.

Williams, J. P. (2005). Instruction in reading comprehension for primary-grade students: A focus on text structure. *The Journal of Special Education, 39*(1), 6–18.

Williams, J. P., Kao, J. C., Pao, L. S., Ordynans, J. G., Atkins, J. G., Cheng, R., & DeBonis, D. (2016). Close analysis of texts with structure (CATS): An intervention to teach reading comprehension to at-risk second graders. *Journal of Educational Psychology, 108*(8), 1061–1077.

Willingham, D. T. (2006). Knowledge in the classroom. *American Educator*, Spring 2006.

Willingham, D. T. (2006/2007). Ask the cognitive scientist: The usefulness of brief instruction in reading comprehension strategies. *American Educator*, Winter 2006/2007, 39–45.

Wright, T. S., & Cervetti, G. N. (2017). A systematic review of the research on vocabulary instruction that impacts text comprehension. *Reading Research Quarterly, 52*(2), 203–226.

Yeari, M., van den Broek, P., & Oudega, M. (2015). Processing and memory of central versus peripheral information as a function of reading goals: Evidence from eye-movements. *Reading and Writing, 28*(8), 1071–1097.

Yuill, N., & Oakhill, J. (1988). Understanding of anaphoric relations in skilled and less skilled comprehenders. *British Journal of Psychology, 79*, 173–186.

Zeno, S., Ivens, S. H., Millard, R. T., & Duvvuri, R. (1995). *The educator's word frequency guide*. Touchstone Applied Science Associates.

Index

A

academic vocabulary, 48–49
Academic Word Finder, 151
accountability, 12, 107, 121, 132–133
   lightweight student, 32, 35–36
   through structured journal, 134–135
Achieve the Core website, 151, 163
Adams, Marilyn, 18, 147
Amos & Boris (William Steig), 51–53
annotation, text, 137–138
antecedents, 69, 120, 149
assessments, 22, 24, 39, 90, 106
   background knowledge and, 29
   standards-based, only annual,
    121–122
author's purpose, 73, 95, 122
autonomous readers, nurtured through
   writing, 133–143
backward design thinking, in textbase
   prep, 115, 153
balanced literacy programs, 18, 22, 149
basal programs, 22, 108, 122

B

Bats at the Beach, 27
Beck, Isabel, 40
Beginning to Read (Marilyn Jager
   Adams), 18
Biemiller, Andrew, 49, 50
Big Words for Young Readers (Heidi Anne
   Mesmer), 56, 152
Birchbark House, The (Louise Erdrich), 47
Bishop, Rudine Sims, 21, 87–88, 151
Blevins, Wiley, 63, 151
Book Basket Project, 151
book baskets, 35
book choice, 35–36
book logs, 34
breadth of vocabulary, 42–45, 49, 54
bridging inferences, 75–78, 83–85, 87

C

celebrating literacy, 12, 23–25, 39,
   144–146, 150
Chall, Jeannie, 39
character analysis, 15, 43, 50–52, 67, 73,
   99, 122
   in close reading, 125, 126
chunking, 117, 135
   of juicy sentences, 141

classroom library, 19, 23, 35, 145, 151
close reading, 54, 85, 111–112, 130, 145
   of *Lety Out Loud* (Angela Cervantes),
    124–129
   teaching, 115–123
   resources about, 153
   system for, 113–114
   writing to support, 133–138
cognates, 51–52, 63, 125
cognitive effort, 85, 87–88, 103, 117
Coherence, Standard of, 7, 89–90, 100,
   129, 133, 134, 143
   attended to, in close reading, 126
   revisiting, 118
coherent texts, for volume reading, 28,
   31
cohesion, 7, 78–81
collective thinking, 95, 118, 119, 133–134,
   145
College and Career Readiness standards,
   114, 115, 121, 123
Common Core State Standards, 67, 114,
   115, 123, 147
complexity, text, 96, 140, 147
   resources about, 153
   in text sets, 28
Concept Oriented Reading Instruction
   (CORI), 23
concrete words, 40, 50, 73, 105, 116, 128
confusion, 93, 124, 146
   as diagnostic tool, 106, 108
   managed through journaling, 134, 136
   stemming from missed connections,
    79–80, 126
connectives, 69, 76–77, 90, 96
   attended to, in close reading, 125, 128
   direct instruction on, 138–140
   in situation model, 83
   types of, 76, 120, 139
   uncertain, 105
continuum of words, for developing
   vocabulary depth, 48
Core Vocabulary Project, 56
Creating Robust Vocabulary (Beck,
   McKeown, Kucan), 51, 53
culture of literacy, 23–25, 146–147, 150
Cunningham, Anne, 28, 31
curiosity, 7, 9, 27, 78, 93, 145–146
   about words, 39, 46, 54, 56–58

D

decoding, 20, 43, 68, 72, 90
decoding, in word analysis routine,
   61–62
depth of vocabulary, 42, 45–48, 54
dictionaries, using, 46, 52
directly teaching words, 46–47, 60, 139
drop-in words, 49–50, 105, 116, 117
   criteria for selecting, 50
   during close reading, 128
   resources about, 153

E

*Educator's Word Frequency Guide,
   The*, 22
effort, cognitive, value of, 85, 87–88,
   103, 117
ELA College and Career Readiness
   standards, 121
ELA curriculum/programs, 44, 49, 68,
   114, 120, 122, 151
11! (Eleven Factorial), 97
English language learners, 14, 84–85
   scaffolding for, 145
equity, educational, 15, 87–88
errors, pedagogical, authors', 12–13,
   147–148
etymology, 45, 56–57, 59, 64
   in action, 62–63
   resources about, 152
   role of, in comprehension, 66
experiences, personal, 24, 26, 86–88,
   90, 103
   in situation model, 69, 81, 83
explaining, 77, 89, 93–95, 109, 130
   in close-reading lesson, 119
exposure to words, 14, 40, 41, 46, 58, 63,
   87–88, 152

F

Family Academy, 8, 18, 20, 21, 38–39, 67,
   131, 138, 144, 147
   close reading in, 113–114
features of text, 96–98, 120, 148–149
feedback, 100, 118, 138
figurative language, attended to, in close
   reading, 125
Fillmore, Lily Wong, 41
   on juicy sentences, 140–141
first read, in close-reading lesson,
   117–118
Free-Choice Reading Tracker, 36

G

General Knowledge Curriculum (GKC), 22–25
Google sheets, for book logs, 34
Goosebumps series, 19
grade-level texts, 18, 22, 28, 92, 129
  misunderstood, 113
  in close reading, 112, 115, 117, 121–123, 129
grouping students, for close-reading lesson, 121
Guthrie, John, 22

H

habits, readers', 57–58, 88, 89, 93
  of attending to words, 46, 47
  cultivated, 118, 146
  structured journaling and, 135
hall passes, for word study, 38–39, 43
Handbook of Reading Research (Cervetti, Wright), 20
Hawkins, Joey, 132
Hiebert, Freddy, 49, 152
high-frequency words, in General Knowledge Curriculum (GKC), 23
high-value words, 51, 63, 116, 122–123, 141, 151
Hirsch, E. D., 21
Hochman, Judith, 139, 152
  on sentence expansion, 142–143
home languages, 14, 51, 63, 122
homework, 36–37

I

independent reading, 25, 34–35, 37, 149
  comprehension and, 72, 109
inferences, making, 76–80
  about "No Spitting" sign, 8–10
  bridging, for situation model, 83–89, 105
information density, 96, 120
informational texts, 19, 27, 36, 82
  journaling about, 136–137
  structures of, 73–75
  Tier 2 words in, 40–41, 45

J

"Jabberwocky" (Lewis Carroll), as example of surface level representation, 72
journaling
  about knowledge, 33, 35
  structured, 134–138, 143
  about words, 47
juicy sentences, 116, 140
  protocol for, 141
  in third read, 122–123

K

kaleidoscopes, frozen, texts as, 96–97, 110
Kintsch, Walter, 28
  his model of comprehension, 7, 71–89

knowing stuff, 24–25, 31
knowledge, 6, 11, 19–20, 30, 66–68
  attended to, in close reading, 125, 127
  celebrating, 23–25
  resources about, 151
  in situation model, 82–88, 103
knowledge building, 20–22, 147
  in third read, 122–123
  prep, for close-reading lesson, 116–117

L

language, oral, 14, 35, 40, 93, 119, 130
language-rich approaches, 14–15, 26
Learn That Word website, 152
Leddy, Diana, 132
lesson planning, for close reading, 115–117
leveled reading, 107, 121, 151
Lexile levels, imprecision of, 129
libraries, 19, 23, 35, 145, 151
lightweight student accountabilities, 32, 35–36
listening, 14, 23, 94, 122, 132, 144, 145, 150
listening comprehension, 104
literature groups, 13, 67–68, 131–132, 145
Lupo, Sarah, 28

M

macro level, 69
macrostructure, of textbase, 73–75, 90
Mae Among the Stars, 27
Magic Tree House series, 19
McKeown, Margaret G., 40, 48, 51, 53, 96, 108, 153
  her forward, 6–7
metacognition, 112
micro level, 69
microstructure, of textbase, 75–81, 90
mighty questions, 119–120
"mirrors, windows, and sliding glass doors," 21, 87–88, 151
Missing May (Rylant), 80, 83–87
mistakes, pedagogical, authors', 12–13, 147–148
Moats, Louisa, 147
model of comprehension, Kintsch, 7, 11, 71–89
monitoring, habits of, 89, 93, 109
  basic, worth teaching (chart), 57
morphemes, 45, 55
morphology, 11, 45, 55–56, 63, 92, 116
  in action, 57–59
  protocol for teaching, 60–62
  resources about, 152
  role of, in comprehension, 66
Mother of All Word Analysis routine, 61–62
motivation, 6, 22, 28
Mr. Morrisey, 34, 47, 58
  his morphology protocol, 60
  his vocabulary routines, 48

multilingual learners (MLs), 14, 15, 90, 110
  juicy sentences and, 141
  close reading for, 112
  cognates and, 61
  connectives and, 76–77, 138, 139
  finding sentence kernels, 142
  knowledge and, 84–85
  language-rich approaches for, 15
  oral exchanges and, 93
  pairing linguistically, 121
  pre-teaching, 117
  preview reading for, 121
  pronoun references and, 120
  scaffolding for, 145
  science topics and, 27
  Tier 3 words and, 41
  using same core texts, 24–25
  word learning and, 51

N

narrative texts, vs. non-narrative, 36, 73–75, 96, 120
  writing about, 136–137, 139

O

obstacles to comprehension, text features as, 76, 110, 119, 120, 125, 128
oral language, 14, 35, 40, 93, 119, 130
orthography, 45
out-of-school reading, 30, 36–37, 41

P

Paterson, Katherine, 131–132
persuasive texts, 74–75
phonemic awareness, 28, 68
phonic patterns, 43, 53, 72
phonics, 20, 28, 63, 66, 150, 151
  in word analysis routine, 61–62
phonology, 45
Placing Text at the Center of the Standards-Aligned ELA Classroom (Meredith Liben and Susan Pimental), 153
prefixes, 55
  basic, worth teaching (chart), 57
prepositions, attended to, in close reading, 125, 142
pre-teaching, 53, 116–117
problem-solution structure, 73–75
pronouns, 69, 79, 120, 149
propositions, 69, 75–76, 138, 149
  attended to, in close reading, 126, 127
  bridging, 78–79, 84–85
  in expanded sentences, 142–143
  parsed in lesson snippet, 102–103
  and text cohesion, 80–81
Proving Your Answer, 94–95, 153
punctuation, 72, 143
  in juicy sentences, 141
  attended to, in close reading, 125
purposes (text feature), 96, 120

Q

question marks, for annotating text, 137
questioning text, 93–95, 109, 114, 146
    in close-reading lesson, 119, 129
    in lesson snippets, 98–106
    about "No Spitting" sign, 8–10
    resources about creating, 153
questions, as diagnostic tools, 95,
    98–106
    mighty, 120

R

Rasinski, Tim, 18
read-alouds, 7, 21, 37, 104, 107, 136, 151
    in close-reading lesson, 117–118, 121,
    127, 128
    for knowledge building, 26–28
    word learning during, 51
Reading Rockets website, 151, 152
relative clauses, 77, 80, 141, 142, 149
repetition (text feature), 80–81, 96, 120
Report of the National Committee on
    Reading, 39
Robust Comprehension Instruction
    with Questioning the Author (Isabel
    L. Beck, Margaret G. McKeown, and
    Cheryl A. Sandora), 153
"Rolling Knowledge Journal," 32–33
roots, 55
    Latin and Greek, 59, 61, 62, 63, 152
Rylant, Cynthia, 18–19, 80, 84–85

S

Scholastic magazines, 28, 151
science of reading (SOR), 6, 12, 43, 64,
    88, 111, 148
science topics, 23, 27, 31, 33, 41, 49, 144
Scott, Katherine, 25
second read, in close-reading lesson,
    118–122
self-explaining, 77, 89, 93–95, 109, 130
self-regulated readers, 95
semantic network, 49, 51, 56, 116
sentence expansion, 142–143
sentence kernels, 141, 142
sentence level, writing at, 138–140
Shanahan, Tim, 109
Seidenberg, Mark, 14
situation model, 7, 69, 81–89, 90
    added in lesson snippet, 102–103
    developed aurally, 104
    fixed in culminating assignments, 123
skills, foundational, 6, 16, 111, 147
small groups, Q&As in, 100
social learning, 94–95, 130, 145–146
    in close-reading lesson, 119
Spanish, 52, 62, 125
spelling, 30, 43, 53, 64
    morphologically (not phonologically),
    63
Standard of Coherence, 7, 89–90, 100,
    133, 134, 143
    in close reading, 126, 129
    revisiting, 118
    strengthened by writing, 133

Stanovich, Keith, 28, 31
strategies, reading, 106–109
structured journaling, 134–138, 143
struggling readers, 6, 24–25, 48, 95, 136
    confusion and, 136
    word analysis and, 61–62
Student Achievement Partners, 33, 114,
    147, 151
suffixes, 55
    basic, worth teaching (chart), 57
surface level of comprehension, 69, 72,
    82, 90, 92, 103, 104
syllabication, in word analysis routine,
    61–62
synonyms, 47, 50, 68
syntax, 11, 68, 89, 96–97, 99, 136
    attended to, in close reading, 125, 127
    in complex sentences, 140–142
    prep, for close-reading lesson, 116

T

teachers, centrality of, 148, 150
Teaching Basic Writing Skills, 139, 152
Teaching Morphology to Improve
    Literacy: A Guide for Teachers (Nikki
    Zeh), 152
Teaching Phonics & Word Study in the
    Intermediate Grades (Wiley Blevins),
    63, 151–152
temporal connectives, 76
text annotation, 137–138
text features, challenging, 96, 120,
    148–149
TextProject site, 152
text selection, for close-reading lesson,
    115
Text Set Project, 35, 151
text sets, 6, 25, 35, 117
    for knowledge building, 27–29
    resources about, 151
    on water (in Rolling Knowledge
    Journal), 33
text structures, 73–75
textbase, 7, 69, 73–81, 90
    example lessons on, 98–106
    prep, for close-reading lesson, 115
textual analysis, 113–114, 145
textual evidence, 93, 110, 112, 123, 130,
    132, 146, 147
    attended to, in close reading, 126
    resources about, 151
third read, in close-reading lesson,
    122–123
thread of a text, losing, 79, 87–88, 99,
    120, 125
Tier 1 words, 40
Tier 2 words, 40–41, 117, 149
    for developing vocabulary breadth,
    44–45
    for developing vocabulary depth, 48
    used as drop ins, 50
    in curriculum, 22, 44–45
Tier 3 words, 41, 62
topics
    focus on, 22, 23, 31, 68

knowledge of, in situation model, 82
    in text sets, 27
    unfamiliar, 96, 120
transitions, 47, 95
    attended to, in close reading, 126, 128
    complexity of, 96, 120
turn-and-talks, 53, 94–95

V

Vermont, Community College of, 134
Vermont Writing Collaborative, 133,
    153–154
visualizing, 8–10, 40, 86, 107
vocabulary, 6–7, 11, 27, 30, 66, 93, 120
    attended to, in close reading, 125, 127,
    128
    breadth of, 42–45, 48
    depth of, 45–48
    prep, for close-reading lesson, 116
    resources about, 151–152
    tiers of, 40–41
volume of reading, 13, 25, 149
    for breadth of Tier 2 vocabulary, 45
    for knowledge building, 28–37

W

Washington, Julie, 14
weak readers, 29, 37, 67
    confusion and, 136
    detoured by strategies, 107–109
Weaver, Kareem, 148
Wexler, Natalie, 139
"What Reading Does for the Mind"
    (Cunningham, Stanovich), 31
Whipple, Guy Montrose, 39
Williams, Joanna, 39
Willingham, Dan, 22, 32, 109, 110
wonderings, students', 26–27, 95, 118
    in structured journal, 134–137
word families, 49, 56, 116
word knowledge, 38–39, 46
Word Nerds (Overturf, Montgomery,
    Smith), 63, 152
word nerds, 47, 48
word recognition, 43, 67–68, 72, 81–82,
    90, 150
"Words We Know a Lot About" chart, 47
Wordsmyth's Children's Dictionary, 52
writing
    activities, 12
    at sentence level, 138–140
    during close reading, 133–134
    instruction, 138–141
    word learning and, 53
Writing for Understanding (Vermont
    Writing Collaborative), 132, 133, 153
Writing Revolution, The (Judith
    Hochman, Natalie Wexler), 139, 142
Writing Revolution website, 153

Z

Zonia's Rain Forest, 27